# OPPOSING VIEWPOINTS® SERIES

# Bioterrorism

# Other Books of Related Interest

## Opposing Viewpoints Series

America's Global Influence

National Security

Rogue Nations

## Current Controversies Series

Domestic Wiretapping

Espionage and Intelligence

Weapons of Mass Destruction

## At Issue Series

Can the War on Terrorism be Won?

National Security

Should Governments Negotiate with Terrorists?

"Congress shall make
no law . . . abridging
the freedom of speech,
or of the press."

*First Amendment to the U.S. Constitution*

The basic foundation of our democracy is the First Amendment guarantee of freedom of expression. The Opposing Viewpoints Series is dedicated to the concept of this basic freedom and the idea that it is more important to practice it than to enshrine it.

# Bioterrorism

*Jacqueline Langwith, Book Editor*

**GREENHAVEN PRESS**
*A part of Gale, Cengage Learning*

GALE
CENGAGE Learning

Detroit • New York • San Francisco • New Haven, Conn • Waterville, Maine • London

Christine Nasso, *Publisher*
Elizabeth Des Chenes, *Managing Editor*

© 2008 Greenhaven Press, a part of Gale, Cengage Learning.

Gale and Greenhaven Press are registered trademarks used herein under license.

*For more information, contact:*
Greenhaven Press
27500 Drake Rd.
Farmington Hills, MI 48331-3535
Or you can visit our Internet site at gale.cengage.com

For product information and technology assistance, contact us at

Gale Customer Support, 1-800-877-4253
For permission to use material from this text or product, submit all requests online at
www.cengage.com/permissions

Further permissions questions can be emailed to permissionrequest@cengage.com

Articles in Greenhaven Press anthologies are often edited for length to meet page requirements. In addition, original titles of these works are changed to clearly present the main thesis and to explicitly indicate the author's opinion. Every effort is made to ensure that Greenhaven Press accurately reflects the original intent of the authors. Every effort has been made to trace the owners of copyrighted material.

Cover photograph reproduced by permission of Panoramic Images/Getty Images.

**LIBRARY OF CONGRESS CATALOGING-IN-PUBLICATION DATA**

Bioterrorism / Jacqueline Langwith, book editor.
p. cm. -- (Opposing viewpoints)
Includes bibliographical references and index.
ISBN-13: 978-0-7377-3990-9 (hardcover)
ISBN-13: 978-0-7377-3991-6 (pbk.)
1. Bioterrorism. I. Langwith, Jacqueline.
HV6433.3.B57 2008
363.325'3--dc22

2008002351

Printed in the United States of America
1 2 3 4 5 6 7 12 11 10 09 08

# Contents

## Chapter 3: How Should the United States Prepare for and Protect Against Bioterrorism?

## Chapter 4: What Anti-Bioterrorism Laws and Policies Should the U.S. Government Have?

# Why Consider Opposing Viewpoints?

> "The only way in which a human being can make some approach to knowing the whole of a subject is by hearing what can be said about it by persons of every variety of opinion and studying all modes in which it can be looked at by every character of mind. No wise man ever acquired his wisdom in any mode but this."
>
> *John Stuart Mill*

In our media-intensive culture it is not difficult to find differing opinions. Thousands of newspapers and magazines and dozens of radio and television talk shows resound with differing points of view. The difficulty lies in deciding which opinion to agree with and which "experts" seem the most credible. The more inundated we become with differing opinions and claims, the more essential it is to hone critical reading and thinking skills to evaluate these ideas. Opposing Viewpoints books address this problem directly by presenting stimulating debates that can be used to enhance and teach these skills. The varied opinions contained in each book examine many different aspects of a single issue. While examining these conveniently edited opposing views, readers can develop critical thinking skills such as the ability to compare and contrast authors' credibility, facts, argumentation styles, use of persuasive techniques, and other stylistic tools. In short, the Opposing Viewpoints Series is an ideal way to attain the higher-level thinking and reading skills so essential in a culture of diverse and contradictory opinions.

In addition to providing a tool for critical thinking, Opposing Viewpoints books challenge readers to question their own strongly held opinions and assumptions. Most people form their opinions on the basis of upbringing, peer pressure, and personal, cultural, or professional bias. By reading carefully balanced opposing views, readers must directly confront new ideas as well as the opinions of those with whom they disagree. This is not to simplistically argue that everyone who reads opposing views will—or should—change his or her opinion. Instead, the series enhances readers' understanding of their own views by encouraging confrontation with opposing ideas. Careful examination of others' views can lead to the readers' understanding of the logical inconsistencies in their own opinions, perspective on why they hold an opinion, and the consideration of the possibility that their opinion requires further evaluation.

## Evaluating Other Opinions

To ensure that this type of examination occurs, Opposing Viewpoints books present all types of opinions. Prominent spokespeople on different sides of each issue as well as well-known professionals from many disciplines challenge the reader. An additional goal of the series is to provide a forum for other, less known, or even unpopular viewpoints. The opinion of an ordinary person who has had to make the decision to cut off life support from a terminally ill relative, for example, may be just as valuable and provide just as much insight as a medical ethicist's professional opinion. The editors have two additional purposes in including these less known views. One, the editors encourage readers to respect others' opinions—even when not enhanced by professional credibility. It is only by reading or listening to and objectively evaluating others' ideas that one can determine whether they are worthy of consideration. Two, the inclusion of such viewpoints encourages the important critical thinking skill of objectively evaluating an author's credentials and bias. This evaluation will illuminate an author's reasons for taking a particular stance on an issue and will aid in readers' evaluation of the author's ideas.

It is our hope that these books will give readers a deeper understanding of the issues debated and an appreciation of the complexity of even seemingly simple issues when good and honest people disagree. This awareness is particularly important in a democratic society such as ours in which people enter into public debate to determine the common good. Those with whom one disagrees should not be regarded as enemies but rather as people whose views deserve careful examination and may shed light on one's own.

Thomas Jefferson once said that "difference of opinion leads to inquiry, and inquiry to truth." Jefferson, a broadly educated man, argued that "if a nation expects to be ignorant and free . . . it expects what never was and never will be." As individuals and as a nation, it is imperative that we consider the opinions of others and examine them with skill and discernment. The Opposing Viewpoints Series is intended to help readers achieve this goal.

*David L. Bender and Bruno Leone,*
*Founders*

# Introduction

> *Natural epidemics of such scourges as smallpox and plague are terrifying enough. But the notion that these and other diseases can be harnessed as weapons of war is even more chilling. While rare, the use of biological weapons dates back centuries, and the recent anthrax attacks have brought home in a harrowing way how much of a role they may play in our present era.*
>
> *Susan Lewis, PBS Nova*

In September 2001, America experienced two sets of terrorist attacks. One occurred on September 11 when four U.S. airplanes were hijacked and crashed into the World Trade Center towers, the U.S. Pentagon, and a Pennsylvania field. The other attacks occurred over the course of several weeks beginning on September 18. In the second set of terror attacks, envelopes full of anthrax, a biological weapon, were sent through the mail to U.S. congressmen and news media outlets. Five people died and seventeen were injured. Before 2001, bioterrorism was an obscure fear for Americans: There had been some isolated incidents of fringe groups deliberately contaminating food with salmonella, but mostly bioterrorism was not considered a major threat.

Although bioterrorism appears as a relatively recent threat to America, it is by no means a new threat in the annals of world history. Herodotus, a Greek historian of the fifth century B.C. described how the Scythian archers of the Black Sea dipped their arrows in a putrescent mixture of human blood, feces, and the decomposed bodies of venomous snakes. Those unfortunate souls who were pierced by a Scythian arrow became poisoned with the bacteria of gangrene and tetanus.

Bioterrorism is the deliberate use of a biological organism—such as a virus or bacterium—as a weapon to debilitate or kill one's enemies in an act of war. Historical documents suggest that the first use of a biological weapon in North America occurred at Fort Pitt (present-day Pittsburgh, PA) in 1763.

After the British defeat of the French at Montreal in 1760, hostilities between the British and the Native Americans intensified. In 1763, Native Americans in the Great Lakes region launched an offensive known as Pontiac's War—for an Ottawa chief—that included attacks on British soldiers and settlers in Fort Detroit (present-day Detroit, MI) and Fort Pitt.

Jeffery Amherst, the commander of British forces in North America during and after the French and Indian War, is implicated in a plot to spread smallpox to the Native Americans at Fort Pitt based on a series of letters between himself and his subordinate Colonel Henry Bouquet. In a letter many historians claim was written on or about June 29, 1763, to Colonel Bouquet, Lord Amherst wrote, "Could it not be contrived to send the Small Pox among those disaffected tribes of Native Americans? We must on this occasion use every stratagem in our power to reduce them."

Bouquet replied that he would try and use infected blankets as a means of introducing the disease among the Native Americans. According to historian Bill Twatio, "it would be difficult to overstate General Jeffrey Amherst's visceral dislike for Indians . . . spreading smallpox, shooting women and children, and murdering prisoners—all became part of Amherst's plan to pacify the frontier." The Amherst letters have been used to support the proposition that the British used biological warfare against native Native American populations. As historian Peter d'Errico contends, "All in all, the letters . . . remove all doubt about the validity of the stories about Lord

Jeff and germ warfare. The General's own letters sustain the stories." However, other historians doubt Amherst's involvement in spreading smallpox. He may have discussed it in correspondence with Bouquet, they say, but there is no evidence that Colonel Bouquet actually carried out Amherst's suggestion. These historians contend that there is evidence showing that such an attack had already been carried out at Fort Pitt prior to the Amherst and Bouquet correspondence. These contentions are supported by the journal of William Trent, commander of the local militia of the townspeople of Pittsburgh during Pontiac's siege of the fort. Trent's entry for June 24, 1763, includes the following statement: "Out of our regard for them, we gave them two blankets and an handkerchief out of the Small Pox Hospital. I hope it will have the desired effect." The officer in charge of Fort Pitt on June 24 was Swissborn British Captain Simeon Ecuyer.

Some historians doubt that either Amherst or Ecuyer could have caused a smallpox outbreak in the Native American community around Fort Pitt. These historians acknowledge that the journal entry of Trent seems to support the claim that under the authority of Captain Ecuyer the Native Americans were given blankets containing smallpox, and Amherst may or may not have known of the specific incident, but he had considered the same thing. However, historical researcher O.N. Eddins, contends that "two blankets would have had little to do with the spread of smallpox among the Indians. A by-far greater source for spreading the smallpox virus would have been infected blood from mutilated soldier and settler bodies, scalps, clothing, and in some cases cannibalism, which occurred during the Pontiac Rebellion." Additionally, historian Philip Ranlet says "plenty of evidence suggests that either the smallpox virus was already dead on the unpleasant gifts [blankets] or that the presents simply failed to fulfill Trent's ardent desire to infect the Indians."

Now, over 200 years later, no one can know for sure whether the British used smallpox as a biological weapon against the Native Americans at Fort Pitt. However, the topic still garners considerable interest and debate. Similarly, since the 2001 anthrax attacks occurred in the United States, the topic of bioterrorism has been written about endlessly, and it is arguable that it will also be discussed years into the future. In *Opposing Viewpoints: Bioterrorism,* the contributors discuss bioterrorism in the following chapters: How Great Is the Threat of Bioterrorism?, What Are the Issues Associated with Biodefense Research?, How Should the United States Prepare for and Protect Against Bioterrorism?, and What Anti-Bioterrorism Policies Should the U.S. Government Have?

OPPOSING
VIEWPOINTS®
SERIES

# CHAPTER 1

# How Great Is the Threat of Bioterrorism?

# Chapter Preface

A virulent blend of the plague and the Ebola virus, a fast-acting and even more deadly version of the human immunodeficiency virus (HIV), and pathogens designed to target specific races or ethnicities; these are examples of potential new biological weapons spawned by advances in recombinant DNA technology. Most current bioterrorism discussions center on the threat posed by smallpox, anthrax, or a host of other centuries-old viruses and bacteria. However, many experts believe that the threat posed by new pathogens genetically engineered using recombinant DNA technology pose the greatest biological threat.

Recombinant DNA technology consists of enzymes, chemicals, and instruments that allow scientists to identify, manipulate, read, and understand genetic information. In 1970, scientists Hamilton Smith and Daniel Nathans discovered that some enzymes act like scissors to cut DNA. Their Nobel prize-winning discovery of what are called "restriction enzymes" paved the way for recombinant DNA technologies that are based on the "cutting and pasting" of genes from one organism into another organism. Since its inception, the field of recombinant DNA has proliferated and has been used to produce mass quantities of human insulin for diabetics, discover the genes that cause cystic fibrosis, certain types of cancer, and many other diseases, and establish paternity, ancestry, and link criminals to crimes (or clear innocent suspects).

Although humankind has benefited immensely from recombinant DNA technology, there has always been a danger associated with it. In 1975, many of the most preeminent scientists in the field of molecular biology held a conference at Asilomar, CA, to discuss fears that a dangerous new organism could be accidentally produced by a combination of genes from two different species. The conference resulted in the establishment of research guidelines to ensure that recombinant DNA research would be performed safely. Over 30 years later, the fear is not so much that a dangerous organism could be accidentally produced. Instead, the fear in the 21st century is that recombinant DNA technology will be used by terrorists to intentionally produce a dangerous biological weapon.

In a 2006 story published in the scientific journal *Technology Review*, journalist Mark Williams describes an interview with former Soviet weapons scientist Serguei Popov. In the 1970s and 1980s, Popov worked for Biopreparat, the main biological warfare agency of the former Soviet Union. According to Williams, in the interview Popov described a Soviet strategy that used recombinant DNA technology to insert deadly viral genes inside a pathogenic bacterium so that medical treatment of a victim's initial symptoms from one microbe would trigger a second microbe's growth. Said Popov, "the first symptom could be plague, and a victim's fever would get treated with something as simple as tetracycline, that tetracycline would itself be the factor inducing expression of a second set of genes, which could be a whole virus or a combination of viral genes." According to Williams, the DNA technologies and instruments used during the 1970s and 1980s when Popov was at Biopreparat were far less sophisticated than they are today. The fact that the Soviets were able to genetically engineer such pathogens back then suggests that anyone who can get their hands on old recombinant DNA equipment could make a new biological weapon. Says Williams, "We live in a world where gene-sequencing equipment bought secondhand on eBay and unregulated biological material delivered in a FedEx package provide the means to create biological weapons."

Some scientists, however, are skeptical that just anyone can create new biological weapons. Scientist Allison Macfarlane says, "Even if terrorists could create new pathogens virulent to humans, it's not at all clear that they could 'weaponize' them—

that is, put the pathogens into a form that is highly infectious to humans and then disperse them in ways that expose large numbers of people." Charles Allen, Chief Intelligence Officer at the Department of Homeland Security agrees. In May 2006, Allen told the U.S. Congressional Committee on Homeland Security, "Just because the technology is available does not mean terrorists can or will use it. In general, terrorist capabilities in the area of bioterrorism are crude and relatively unsophisticated . . . we would expect to see use of traditional biological agents before the appearance of advanced biological weapon agents."

Many people are concerned that recombinant DNA technology could be used as an ethnic or race-based biological weapon. An ethnic biological weapon sometimes referred to as a "genetic bomb," aims to harm only or primarily persons of specific ethnicities or genetic profiles. Some scientists say it's possible to construct pathogens that recognize certain genetic sequences that occur only or primarily in the genomes (i.e. the entire set of genetic information) of certain races or ethnicities. Only people with the genetic sequence would be vulnerable to the pathogen. Some people think this could be pushed even further and pathogens could be constructed to recognize and infect people with certain physical characteristics, for instance blue eyes, brown eyes, or almond-shaped eyes.

Others say the concerns are exaggerated. "Trying to find a weapon that affects quite a few of one ethnic group and none of another ethnic group is just not going to happen," says David Goldstein, who studies population genetics at University College London. "Because all groups are quite similar, you will never get something that is highly selective. The best you would probably do is something that kills 20 percent of one group and 28 percent of another."

As the debates about recombinant DNA technology and genetically engineered pathogens demonstrate, there are diverse views regarding the threat posed by different kinds of biological weapons. The authors of the viewpoints in the following chapter provide their opinions on the magnitude of the bioterrorism threat.

VIEWPOINT 1

> *"The anthrax letters of 2001 were an entirely new phenomenon. They moved the threat of bioterrorism, which had previously been mostly theoretical, closer to reality."*

# Bioterrorism Poses a Significant Threat

*Jason Pate and Gary Ackerman*

*In the following viewpoint, Jason Pate and Gary Ackerman of the Center for Nonproliferation Studies (CNS) contend that the threat of a bioterrorist attack against the United States is very real. They say that the anthrax attacks that occurred in 2001, as well as revelations about the al Qaeda terrorist network, demonstrate that a bioterrorist attack in the United States is possible and could result in vast numbers of casualties. Pate and Ackerman propose preparation measures the United States should take to mitigate the effects of such an attack. The CNS at the Monterey Institute of International Studies and the Nuclear Threat Initiative (NTI) are nongovernmental organizations devoted to reducing the spread of nuclear, biological, and chemical weapons.*

Jason Pate, Gary Ackerman, "Assessing the Threat of Mass-Casualty Bioterrorism," *Center for Nonproliferation Studies (CNS), Monterey Institute of International Studies,* October, 2001. Reproduced by permission. Available at www.nti.org/e_research/ e3_1a.html.

As you read, consider the following questions:

1. According to the authors, what types of weapons are commonly called "weapons of mass destruction (WMDs)?"

2. According to the authors, the anthrax attacks of 2001 represented the first time that what was sent through the mail? Be specific.

3. According to the authors, the anthrax attacks of 2001 made it abundantly clear that one of the key components of U.S. national security should be what?

The September 11 attacks and the subsequent anthrax letters, combined with evidence of al-Qai'da's interest in toxic agents, have focused renewed attention on the possibility of terrorism involving chemical, biological, radiological, or nuclear weapons, commonly called weapons of mass destruction (WMD). WMD terrorism is not a new phenomenon: In March 1995, the Japanese doomsday cult Aum Shinrikyo released sarin nerve agent in the Tokyo subway, killing 12 and injuring over 1,000. This incident, perpetrated by an apocalyptic group seeking to inflict mass casualties, demonstrated that at least some terrorist groups are capable of acquiring and using chemical weapons. Mass-casualty terrorism is also not new to the United States. In April 1995, a truck bomb destroyed the Alfred P. Murrah Federal Building in Oklahoma City, killing 168 and injuring more than 700. Perpetrated by a lone actor influenced by right-wing ideology, this unprecedented attack brought the threat of mass-casualty terrorism—albeit with conventional explosives—to the American heartland.

## New Era of Terrorism

In the aftermath of these events, some analysts declared that a new era of terrorism had emerged, one involving a sea-change in terrorist tactics and goals. With religion arguably replacing politics as the primary ideological motivation for terrorist groups, it was possible to envision terrorist groups, relatively unconstrained by societal norms, seeking to perpetrate more extreme acts of violence than more "traditional" terrorist organizations. For example, Usama bin Laden, the alleged mastermind of the September 11 attacks, the 1999 bombing of the USS Cole in Yemen, and the 1998 near-simultaneous bombings of the U.S. embassies in Kenya and Tanzania, openly declared an interest in acquiring WMD for attacks against American targets; more recently, alleged members of his organization have been apprehended with dangerous poisons. At the same time, the spread of dual-use technologies and WMD-relevant materials to state-sponsors of terrorism and the lack of controls on weapons materials and know-how in the former Soviet Union have raised serious concerns about the increasing threat of terrorists acquiring and using WMD. This is especially relevant in the context of increasing tensions and possible conflict between the United States and countries that have developed WMD and have supported terrorist groups in the past, such as Iraq and North Korea.

## The Anthrax Attacks and Bioterrorism

The anthrax letters of 2001 were an entirely new phenomenon. They moved the threat of bioterrorism, which had previously been mostly theoretical, closer to reality. Despite hundreds of anthrax hoaxes in the few years prior to October 2001, the anthrax letters represented the first time that actual, virulent anthrax spores were sent through the mail. The attacks were scattered, isolated incidents targeted at prominent media and political figures, but also resulted in a number of people, notably postal workers and congressional staff, suffering from collateral exposure. One of the most significant aspects is that, thus far, the perpetrator remains at-large.

There have been conflicting reports from various government agencies regarding the quality of the anthrax used in the attacks. It may have been highly sophisticated: milled to a fine powder and treated with chemical additives to keep the spores from clumping and becoming weighed down by humidity, so that they aerosolize more readily.

## The Perpetrators

The fact that the anthrax may have been milled to a fine powder and mixed with chemicals—techniques involving specialized military knowledge unlikely to be available to laboratory microbiologists—suggests that the perpetrator(s) may have been involved at one point in time with the biological weapons program of a state—perhaps even a scientist who worked on the former U.S. biological weapons program. Although the chemical additives are readily available, the critical skill is knowing which additives to use, and how and when to use them.

These findings are consistent with a number of hypotheses: the perpetrators were aided by a foreign state, were assisted by scientists who once worked in a state-level bioweapons program, or purchased the anthrax on the international black market. The FBI has released only a vague profile of the perpetrator(s), as most probably male, with a scientific background and an intimate knowledge of Trenton, New Jersey.

The fact that the same strain of anthrax appears to have been used in the letter attacks directed against individuals in Florida, New York, and Washington, D.C. also suggests that this is a coordinated effort by a single individual (i.e., a biological Unabomber), a small domestic group, or a large network such as al-Qai'da. Still, the identity of the perpetrator or perpetrators remains unclear. Some evidence, such as the quality of the anthrax, points to an international source, but other evidence points in the direction of domestic terrorists.

## Mass-Casualty Terrorism

According to terrorism scholar Bruce Hoffman, until September 11, 2001, fewer than 1,000 Americans had been killed in terrorist attacks in the United States or abroad since 1968. The quantum leap in casualties—with more than 3,000 dead—is particularly alarming in terms of terrorist motivations. Terrorist trends have suggested an increase in casualties per incident, and the September 11 attacks appear to conform to this pattern. However, the anthrax incidents have been small in scale, with the apparent intent of frightening rather than killing large numbers of people.

It is possible that the perpetrators of the anthrax attacks had only a limited amount of powdered anthrax spores—enough to deliver in small amounts through the mail, but not enough to disseminate through the air as an aerosol cloud that could infect large numbers of people. They may also not have been motivated to inflict mass casualties, even if they could. Critics have also pointed out the significant technical hurdles to the use of chemical or biological weapons to cause massive numbers of casualties. Despite Aum Shinrikyo's vast financial resources and scientific expertise, it was unable to perpetrate mass-casualty attacks with either chemical or biological weapons. In any case, large numbers of casualties can be caused by terrorists without resorting to WMD. The September 11 terrorists did not require advanced weaponry to cause mass casualties and mass destruction. They used a low-technology operation and returned to decades-old terrorist tactics—hijacking planes—to achieve their goals.

One thing that the 2001 anthrax attacks made abundantly clear is that public health is a key component of U.S. national security. The anthrax attacks revealed serious gaps in the public health system, particularly at the state and local levels. Fortunately, alert physicians diagnosed the early cases correctly. One would hope that the attacks served as a lesson to public health officials by putting them on guard for the possibility of a covert bioterrorist attack, thus lessening the impact of any future attack. Yet many other doctors and health departments in other cities and towns around the country are not prepared to recognize or contain a bioterrorist attack. These gaps must be remedied immediately if the country is to be prepared for more serious threats. Indeed, improving the public health infrastructure will help address the threat posed by bioterrorism as well as the arguably much greater threat from emerging infectious diseases.

The silver lining of the current dark cloud is that there is a window of opportunity to improve our preparedness for a larger-scale biological attack. It is important, however, to address these vulnerabilities in a systematic and determined way, rather than continuing to ride the sine wave of alarmism and complacency that has plagued earlier efforts to improve domestic preparedness.

U.S. policymakers must also be prepared for an entirely different type of attack. If terrorists have access to a significant manufacturing capability, the United States must be prepared for the possibility of an escalation from targeted attacks to mass-casualty attacks with powdered anthrax or some other agent. The most ominous, but not the most likely, threat would involve the deliberate release of a contagious agent, such as pneumonic plague or smallpox. The health system would then have to detect and contain the outbreak before it spread widely.

Concerns about mass-casualty bioterrorism have again been raised in connection with Usama bin Laden's al-Qai'da group. Uncorroborated testimony in a high-profile Egyptian trial in 1999 indicated that al-Qai'da had acquired dangerous biological agents such as the anthrax bacterium, the Ebola virus, salmonella, and botulinum toxin, while other reports mentioned plague and ricin. al-Qai'da's purported research efforts were focused on weaponizing anthrax, and U.S. forces discovered a partially built biological weapons lab near Kandahar that was designed to produce anthrax even though no actual agents were found. There is still no conclusive evidence that al-Qai'da succeeded in weaponizing any of these agents.

# Preparing for Mass-Casualty Bioterrorism

## The Threat Is Growing Larger

The threat of a biological weapons attack is large and rapidly growing larger, but our capability to respond is lagging far behind. If an attack is a contagious disease, an international response will be necessary to avoid illness and death on a large scale and to limit social, economic and political aftershocks. Medicines and vaccines will need to be developed, refined, produced, and distributed to bring an end to the event as well as to reduce the effects of a repeat attack.

*Gigi Kwik Gronvall, "Statement Delivered at the Sixth Review Conference of the Biological Weapons Convention," November 21, 2006. Available at www.upmc-biosecurity.org.*

However, in January 2003, traces of the toxin ricin was found in an apartment in London used by a group of men potentially linked to al-Qai'da. . . .

Preventing mass-casualty terrorism with WMD agents and, if prevention fails, managing the consequences of an attack, is an enormously demanding task. Since 1995, the United States has allocated enormous resources to combating WMD terrorism. Numerous government programs have been created in an effort to prevent and deter terrorism or to mitigate the effects of a major attack. These efforts have focused on enhancing the ability of local first-responders to decontaminate and treat survivors, augmented by additional capabilities at the state and federal levels. But analysts have criticized the significant overlap and redundancy among various federal counterterrorism programs, as well as the lack of a clear strategy for integrating these diverse elements into a coherent whole. The events of September 11 and the subsequent anthrax attacks have also contributed to these efforts. President Bush, together with Congress, created a new government agency, the Department of Homeland Security, in an effort to ensure greater coordination in response and intelligence collaboration.

Planning domestic preparedness requires coordinating not only some 40 federal agencies, but also a large number of state and local agencies, as well as important elements of the private sector. The creation of the Department of Homeland Security is a useful first step, but the department's head, Tom Ridge [Michael Chertoff replaced Ridge in 2005] will have to overcome budgetary bottlenecks and chronic turf battles among rival federal bureaucracies.

In order to be prepared for a range of contingencies, the first line of defense is to train doctors to recognize the effects of a variety of biological threat agents, and to establish clear channels of communication among primary care physicians and local health departments, as well as among local, state, and federal public health officials. These various levels must be integrated by e-mail and other communications networks into a seamless web. Diagnostic laboratories around the country also need to have the appropriate tests to identify exotic disease agents such as anthrax in patient specimens. Finally, national distribution mechanisms for drugs and vaccines must be developed so that an outbreak of disease can be contained rapidly. The private sector, such as the U.S. chemical industry, transportation, energy, telecommunications infrastructure, and food companies, will also need to spend more to ensure the safety and security of their products and services.

The optimal approach to WMD terrorism is prevention, rather than consequence mitigation. U.S. counterterrorism efforts designed to address this threat have generally been developed in the absence of a realistic assessment of terrorist motivations and technical capabilities for using WMD. To the extent possible, intelligence collection and analysis capabilities must be strengthened to assess the ability of terrorists to acquire, produce, and deliver biological and chemical agents. Improved capabilities are needed to distinguish between natural and deliberate outbreaks of disease. These new challenges will require the intelligence community to improve its depth of expertise in microbiology, chemistry, and epidemiology.

*"'Bioterrorism' may or may not develop into a serious concern in the future, but it is not one of the most pressing problems that we have on the planet today."*

# The Threat of Bioterrorism Is Exaggerated

## Milton Leitenberg

*In the following viewpoint, Milton Leitenberg assesses the threat of bioterrorism and finds it is not as great a threat as many U.S. government officials allege. Leitenberg lists several threats to humankind that he says are more imminent and pressing than bioterrorism, such as the threat of chemical terrorism and pandemic flu outbreak. He says U.S. government officials and others are deliberately exaggerating the bioterrorism threat, and this is a grave mistake. Milton Leitenberg is a leading expert on biological weapons and arms control. He has authored almost two hundred papers and several books on the issue.*

Milton Leitenberg, "Assessing the Biological Weapons and Bioterrorism Threat" *Strategic Studies Institute of the U.S. Army War College.* Reproduced by permission. Available at www.strategicstudiesinstitute.army.mil/pubs/display.cfm?PubID=639.

As you read, consider the following questions:

1. According to Leitenberg, how many people are infected with "falciparium malaria," and how many people are at risk worldwide?

2. According to Leitenberg, the interval between flu pandemics is usually about how many years?

3. According to Leitenberg, until the perpetrator(s) of the 2001 anthrax attacks are identified, it will be impossible to do what?

Speaking at the World Economic Forum in Davos, Switzerland, on January 27, 2005, U.S. Senate Majority Leader William Frist stated that "The greatest existential threat we have in the world today is biological." He added the prediction that "an inevitable bio-terror attack" would come "at some time in the next 10 years." He was seconded by Dr. Tara O'Toole, head of the Center for Biosecurity at the University of Pittsburgh: "This [bioterrorism] is one of the most pressing problems we have on the planet today."

Are these statements realistic?

Are they even proximately realistic?

## Competing Threats to Humankind

By way of the most cursory comparison, one can set potential bioterrorism against:

Global climate change, which could affect populations in every corner of the globe, alter the current growth cycles of food crops that have evolved over millennia, and consequently food production;

Ocean quality deterioration, deforestation, desertification, depletion of fresh-water aquifers—all of these are also global in impact;

The complex of global population growth, food production, energy and other resource constraints, and the waste products—solid, liquid and gaseous—produced by human society and the impact of these on regional and global ecosystems;

Between 224.5 and 236 million people died in the 20th century in wars and conflict—say, roughly 230 million. This early in the 21st century, it is impossible to say whether the harvest of conflict-related deaths will be any different in the 21st century than it was in the 20th century.

If one adds deaths due to poverty, the figures become astronomical. Jeffrey Sachs currently estimates this sum worldwide at 20,000 people per day, or 7.3 million per year, approximately 75 million over a 10-year period. Some portion of the deaths that Sachs counts may be due to treatable disease: these are discussed separately below.

A working group convened by the Strategic Assessments Group of the Central Intelligence Agency (CIA) and the RAND Corporation in September 2004 listed 10 "future national security threats . . . to the United States" looking ahead to 2020. Of the 10, one was "proliferation of weapons of mass destruction (WMD)" and a second was "new health threats, such as severe acute respiratory syndrome (SARS)." There was no mention of the use of biological weapons by a terrorist group.

Turning to the 1999 Millennium Project list of "The 15 Global Challenges We Face at the Millennium," only 1 of the 15 dealt with disease agents: "What can be done to reduce the threat of new and reemerging diseases, and the increasing number of immune micro-organisms." It did not include consideration of "bio-terrorism" at all.

Within a 10-day period between April 6 and April 16, 2005, no fewer than five other competitors were announced as being the most dire threat faced by nations:

- nuclear terrorism;

- 640 million small arms and light weapons around the world, which are responsible for an estimated 300,000 deaths per year;

- a terrorist attack using high explosives aimed at cooling ponds holding stored irradiated nuclear reactor rods at civil nuclear power plants, leading to reactor core melt-down and radiation release analogous to the Chernobyl reactor disaster;

- the possibility of impact of an asteroid with the earth; and

- a missile attack that would detonate a nuclear explosive over the United States producing an Electromagnetic Pulse (EMP) ". . . that could come not only from terrorist organizations like al Queda but from rogue nations such as Iran or North Korea."

To complete the picture, Rogelio Pfirter, Director General of the United Nations Organization for the Prohibition of Chemical Weapons, stated, perhaps unsurprisingly, that ". . . chemical terrorism has been identified in different regions of the world as the number one potential threat."

If one looks only at disease and other human public health concerns, we see the following:

## Disease Threatens to Kill Millions

Three diseases alone—malaria, tuberculosis, and human immuno-deficiency virus/acquired immune deficiency syndrome (HIV/AIDS)—kill 5 million people globally year in, year out. In 2004, that sum reportedly reached 6 million. In 1 decade, that is 50 million dead. And although the contribution of HIV/AIDS to this sum is more recent, the overall total has apparently been roughly the same for many years past. Projected HIV/AIDS mortality estimates are available for the decade to come, and will very likely produce another 50 million dead due to these three diseases. Falciparium malaria is estimated to currently infect 515 million people worldwide, with 2.2 billion people—one out of every three people in the world—at risk of infection. The cost of ma-

## Exaggeration of Threat Is Irresponsible

Although it makes sense to prepare for the possibility of a bioweapons attack, it is irresponsible to loudly assert the certain inevitability of catastrophic bioterrorism. Such talk will undermine the nation's ability to minimize panic and ensure public trust and cooperation in the event of an attack. It also promotes malevolent interest in and public tolerance of bioweapons.

*Alan Pearson, "Bioweapons," Issues in Science and Technology,*
*Spring, 2005. Available at www.issues.org.*

laria to the economy of African nations alone is estimated at $12 billion per year. Malaria is preventable or treatable. Tuberculosis currently infects nearly 1 billion people, and 1 billion new cases are anticipated by 2020, 35 million of whom will die. . . .

## Pandemic Flu Outbreak

WHO officials have been warning for years of the imminence of a pandemic flu outbreak. They have warned that the pandemic was "almost inevitable," and long overdue. There were three influenza pandemics in the 20th century. The worst was the 1918–19 "Spanish flu." Estimates of the mortality it caused range from a low of 20 million to higher estimates of over 50 million worldwide and even 100 million. The Asian flu of 1957–58 killed about 1 million people globally, while the third flu pandemic, the 1968–79 Hong Kong flu, killed an estimated 1-4 million people.

Flu pandemics usually occur about every 20 to 30 years, and it has now been 40 years since the last one. The H5N1 avian flu strain, which first appeared in the 1997 Hong Kong outbreak, is still believed to be generally incapable of person-to-person transmission. Until very recently, the human lethality of the H5N1 strain was considered to be approximately 50 percent of those infected. However, it is now understood that the actual incidence of infection is substantially higher. . . .

In all of the above, which has been by way of introduction, two groups of global problems faced by humankind are listed. The second group enumerates only a few pathogen and public-health problems, with an annual mortality of above 11 million people per year. So, is bioterrorism "the greatest existential threat we have in the world today"? And is it "one of the most pressing problems we have on the planet today"?

No. Absolutely not. That is clearly demonstrated by the above examples. . . .

> "Bioterrorism" may or may not develop into a serious concern in the future, but it is *not* "one of the most pressing problems that we have on the planet today."

## Threat from Other Countries and Terrorists Reduced

> The number of state BW [biological weapons] programs has apparently been reduced by one-third or one-fourth in the past 15 years. The remaining number of countries appears to be stable; no compensating rise in offensive state BW programs has been identified. In addition, the U.S. Government—which has almost without exception in past decades been the only country to publicly identify WMD proliferants—appears in its most recent statements to be qualifying the status of states with presumed offensive BW programs. To date, no state is known to have assisted any nonstate or terrorist group to obtain biological weapons.

> The production and distribution of a dry powder anthrax product in the United States in 2001 is the most significant event. However, understanding to what degree that demonstration of competence is relevant to "traditional" terrorist groups is impossible until the perpetrator(s) of the anthrax

events are identified. If it was done with assistance, materials, knowledge, access, etc., derived from the U.S. biodefense program, the implications change entirely.

The Rajneesh group (1984) succeeded in culturing Salmonella. The Japanese Aum Shinrikyo group failed to obtain, produce, or disperse anthrax and botulinum toxin. The steps taken by the al-Qaida group in efforts to develop a BW program were more advanced than the United States understood prior to its occupation of Afghanistan in November–December 2001. Nevertheless, publicly available information, including the somewhat ambiguous details that appeared in the March 31, 2005, report of the Commission on Intelligence Capabilities, indicates that the group failed to obtain and work with pathogens. Should additional information become available regarding the extent to which the al-Qaida BW effort had progressed, that assessment might have to be changed.

## Terrorists Unsuccessful in Working with Pathogens

Scenarios for national BW exercises that posit various BW agents in advanced states of preparation in the hands of terrorist groups simply disregard the requirements in knowledge and practice that such groups would need in order to work with pathogens. Unfortunately, 10 years of widely broadcast public discussion has provided such groups, at least on a general level, with suggestions as to what paths to follow. If and when a nonstate terrorist group does successfully reach the stage of working with pathogens, there is every reason to believe that it will involve classical agents, without any molecular genetic modifications. Preparing a dry powder preparation is likely to prove difficult, and dispersion to produce mass casualties equally so. Making predictions on the basis of what competent professionals may find "easy to do" has been a common error and continues to be so. The utilization of molecular genetic technology by such groups is still further off in time. No serious military threat assessment imputes to opponents capabilities that they do not have. There is no justification for imputing to real world terrorist groups capabilities in the biological sciences that they do not posess.

## Deliberate Exaggeration

For the past decade the risk and immanence of the use of biological agents by nonstate actors/terrorist organizations—"bioterrorism"—has been systematically and deliberately exaggerated. It became more so after the combination of the 9/11 events and the October–November 2001 anthrax distribution in the United States that followed immediately afterwards. U.S. Government officials worked hard to spread their view to other countries. An edifice of institutes, programs, conferences, and publicists has grown up which continue the exaggeration and scare-mongering. In the last year or two, the drumbeat had picked up. It may however become moderated by the more realistic assessment of the likelihood of the onset of a natural flu pandemic, and the accompanying realization that the U.S. Government has been using the overwhelming proportion of its relevant resources to prepare for the wrong contingency.

Others see exaggeration as necessary in order to prompt preparation. They acknowledge the exaggeration but argue that political action, the expenditure of public funds for bioterrorism prevention and response programs, will not occur without it. "Bioterrorism" may come someday if societies survive all their other impending crises. However, the persistent exaggeration is not benign: it is almost certainly the single greatest factor in provoking interest in BW among terrorist groups, to the degree that it currently exists, for example, in the al-Qaida organization. Precisely this occurred: Their most senior leadership was provoked by statements regarding bioterrorism and its supposed ease by U.S. officials in 1996–97.

| *"The food supply is by far the most vulnerable to a bioterrorism attack."*

# Bioterrorism Threatens the U.S. Food Supply

*Kevin Coleman*

*In the following viewpoint, Kevin Coleman asserts that the U.S. food supply chain is vulnerable to a terrorist attack. Coleman says there are many points along the food and water supply chains where terrorists could disrupt or contaminate food and water supplies and cause psychological distress, economic disruption, and death. Coleman believes the use of advanced communication and monitoring technology is necessary in order to prevent attacks and safeguard the U.S food and water supply. Kevin Coleman of Technolytics writes a homeland security column for* Directions Magazine.

As you read, consider the following questions:

1. Describe the three types of terrorist attacks that Coleman says are threats to the U.S. food supply.

2. According to Coleman, factory farms make up what percentage of total farms and provide what percentage of output?

Kevin Coleman, "Bioterrorism and the Food Supply," *Directions Magazine*. October 1, 2004. Reproduced by permission. Available at www.directionsmag.com/article.php ?article_id=667&trv=1.

3. According to Coleman, the Support Anti-Terrorism by Fostering Effective Technologies (SAFETY) Act provides what?

The goal of terrorists is to strike fear in the hearts of their targets. This can take many forms. They may wish to cause death, shock, economic disruption, loss of faith in authorities, psychological trauma, dread, or just uncertainty. Perhaps the act that would most readily accomplish this would be an attack on the United States' food supply. Protecting the food supply has been a priority for public health officials for decades. Traditionally, industry and regulators have depended on spot-checks of manufacturing conditions and random sampling of final products to ensure safe food. This system is seen as more reactive than preventive because it finds problems after they have occurred rather than as the food is being prepared.

So what is at stake? Here are some interesting statistics about the food supply-chain in the United States. These are just from the Mid-Atlantic region.

## Mid-Atlantic Food Supply

- Number of farms = over 100,000

- Number of post-farm businesses = nearly 150,000

- Private Sector Food Business = over 12% of private sector businesses involve food

- Collective Sales = over $300 billion

- Employment = nearly 12% of the workforce

The introduction by terrorists of noxious or lethal materials into foods or beverages could result in undetected, rapid and widespread distribution within the food supply-chain that relies on distributed food production, processing and transportation firms. There are really three types of terrorist threats to the food supply.

1. The use of food or water as a delivery mechanism for pathogens, chemicals, and/or other harmful substances for the purpose of causing human illness or death.

2. The introduction of anti-crop or anti-livestock agents into agricultural systems.

3. The physical disruption of the flow of food/water as a result of the destruction of transportation or other vital infrastructure.

## Vulnerability of Food Supply Chain

So how vulnerable is our food supply? That is a question that has been asked by scientists and government officials. The answer lies in an analysis of the "food" supply-chain. The supply chain begins with a vast number of producers (farms) and the numerous transportation, processing and distribution facilities that are all part of bringing the food to the point of consumption. It is estimated that 98 percent of all U.S. farms are family farms. This small, highly distributed food production network creates security, monitoring and tracking challenges. Very large factory farms make up only 3 percent of the total farms but contribute more than 40 percent of the output. In addition to being vulnerable to terrorist attacks, this system makes it exceedingly difficult to trace back and identify the source of the contaminated food. . . .

Four recent GAO [Government Accounting Office] reports found gaps in federal controls for protecting agriculture and the food supply. Local, state and federal officials must do even more to protect our food supply from tampering. A new comprehensive approach is needed if we are to safeguard our food supply.

- Document the "food" supply-chain

- Analyze risks and vulnerabilities

- Identify critical control points

- Establish monitoring procedures

- Develop response plan

- Develop reporting and tracking system

- Develop system reliability checks

The Public Health Security and Bioterrorism Preparedness and Response Act of 2002 (the Bioterrorism Act) directs the Secretary of Health and Human Services to take steps to protect the public from a threatened or actual terrorist attack on the U.S. food supply.

Exempt from these regulations are the transportation vehicles that hold food only in the usual course of business. As you could imagine the ability to attack our food supply while in transit from the production site is a critical area and possibly the area that has the least amount of protection currently. It is important to recognize that this is only one of many exceptions granted under the act.

Protecting U.S. agriculture and ensuring safe and wholesome meat and poultry is one of the primary challenges facing [United States Department of Agriculture] USDA. The office of the Inspector General of the United States Department of Agriculture's chief missions is to ensure the safety of the food supply, both by auditing food safety programs to detect deficiencies and recommend improvements and by investigating criminal activity involving the intentional contamination of food products. They also monitor the processing and sale of adulterated meat, poultry, and egg products; and the substitution, adulteration or other misrepresentation of food products regulated or inspected by the USDA.

## Applying Technology to the Threat

The Department of Homeland Security [DHS] in June 2004 announced the first Designations and Certifications under the Support Anti-terrorism by Fostering Effective Technologies

## Agroterrorism a National Security Threat

The potential of terrorist attacks against agricultural targets (agroterrorism) is increasingly recognized as a national security threat, especially after the events of September 11, 2001. Agroterrorism is a subset of bioterrorism, and is defined as the deliberate introduction of an animal or plant disease with the goal of generating fear, causing economic losses, and/or undermining social stability.

The goal of agroterrorism is not to kill cows or plants. These are the means to the end of causing economic damage, social unrest, and loss of confidence in government. Human health could be at risk if contaminated food reaches the table or if an animal pathogen is transmissible to humans (zoonotic). While agriculture may not be a terrorist's first choice because it lacks the "shock factor" of more traditional terrorist targets, many analysts consider it a viable secondary target.

*Jim Monke, "Agroterrorism: Threats and Preparedness,"*
CRS Report for Congress, *updated August 25, 2006.*

(SAFETY) Act. The SAFETY Act provides liability limitations for makers and sellers of qualified anti-terrorism technologies, including those that may be used to protect the nation's food supply. DHS is also developing a new National Biodefense Analysis and Countermeasures Center (NBACC) to support the law enforcement and intelligence communities in their biodefense responsibilities. The Center will apply the newest advances in science to the challenges both of biological threat characterization and of bioforensics, strengthening the nation's ability to determine the source of a biological agent used in an attack and strengthening deterrence. In June 2004, DHS announced its new Regional Technology Integration (RTI) initiative. RTI provides a mechanism for working directly with urban areas on infrastructure protection (including protection of the food supply) to develop and deliver new technologies as part of a regional security response. The program focuses on regional collaboration, private sector solutions, measurable objectives and continuous evaluation, and communicating best practices and lessons learned to other communities, states, Congress, the Administration, and other federal agencies.

The support is there. Now all that is needed is a workable platform that can provide an economically feasible solution to safeguarding our food supply. A critical component of this platform will, without question, be a GIS system that supports tracking and traceability. Incorporated into the platform will also be RFID capabilities to trace the product throughout the food supply-chain. These hybrid tags will also serve to detect tampering and integrated with new biosensors will alert food processors to possible contaminates. But this platform will not be cheap. The question is can the platform be developed and implemented in time to protect the population from a bioterrorist attack against our food supply? Only time will answer that question.

## We Must Act to Protect Our Food Supply

The food supply is by far the most vulnerable to a bioterrorism attack. This year we learned from news reports that terrorists have developed materials to manufacture salmonella and botulinum, and they may have intended to poison the food supply. Even more alarming was a *Washington Post* article on biological weapons developed by the South African government under the apartheid-regime, including a biological agent created by splicing a common strain of E.coli with a toxin-producing gene from Clostridium perfringens. These are only a handful of examples of food bioterrorism that demonstrate the health and economic damage that could be inflicted through an attack on the food supply.

We need to continue to strengthen our food supply surveillance systems and improve communication and coordination among local, state and federal agencies to heighten the ability to recognize and quickly respond to food-borne outbreaks. This will not be cheap or able to be accomplished in a short period of time.

*"Much of the damage agroterrorism is expected to cause is already a reality."*

# Bioterrorism Does Not Pose an Increased Threat to the U.S. Food Supply

*Stan Cox*

*In the following viewpoint, Stan Cox contends that terrorists needn't bother contaminating the U.S. food and water supply. Beef and pork are already contaminated with pathogens that sicken millions of Americans each year. Rivers, streams, and wells are full of nitrates and other chemicals leaching from agricultural operations, and crops are full of toxic pesticides that could cause cancer, neurologic diseases, and infertility. Cox thinks terrorism is the least of concerns to U.S. agriculture. Stan Cox is a plant breeder and writer in Salina, KS. Counterpunch is a biweekly liberal newsletter.*

As you read, consider the following questions:

1. According to Cox, how many times are the terms "agroterrorism" or "terrorism" referenced in the Current Research Information System (CRIS) database from 1998–2001? From 2001–2005?

Stan Cox, "Lurking in the Feedlots of America: 'Agroterrorists' Needn't Bother," *Counterpunch.org*. December 15, 2005. Reproduced by permission. Available at www.counterpunch.org/cox12152005.html.

2. According to Cox and federal Centers for Disease Control and Prevention (CDC) estimates, how many Americans are sickened because of foodborne illnesses annually? How many die?

3. Why are antibiotics fed to livestock even when they aren't sick, according to Cox?

"In the war on terrorism, the fields and pastures of America's farmland might seem at first to have nothing in common with the towers of the World Trade Center or busy seaports. In fact, however, they are merely different manifestations of the same high-priority target, the American economy."

That's United States Senator Susan Collins (R-ME) warning us about "agroterrorism", a specter that she and others in Washington say is stalking rural America. Here in the Great Plains, we're all being exhorted to keep a round-the-clock lookout for agroterrorists lurking around farms or feedlots.

Senator Pat Roberts of Kansas, Republican chair of the Intelligence Committee, has been hyping agroterrorism since 1999. But it took the 9/11 attacks to get some action. Roberts recently told the *Wichita Eagle*, "At least now, when I talk about agroterrorism, people don't tell me to talk about something else."

## "Terrorism" Used to Draw Attention and Funding

Keeping in mind that terrorists never seem inclined to take targeting suggestions from US politicians, we know these days to treat any use the word "terrorism" with deep skepticism. But when a prefix is attached, we should be especially wary.

Given the lack of standardization (the prefix of "bioterrorism" denoting the means of attack, of "narcoterrorism" the means of finance, of "ecoterrorism" the beneficiary, and of "agroterrorism" the target) it's clear that "terrorism" is simply a device to draw attention to whatever is in the prefix, and maybe scare up some funding.

The Current Research Information System (CRIS) is a database describing all agricultural research projects funded by the US Department of Agriculture through grants, contracts, or its own agencies. A search of CRIS for variants of the terms "agroterrorism" or "terrorism" turns up 18 agriculture-related projects initiated during the four-year period 1998–2001. For the following four years, 2001–05, there are precisely 100 projects that mention terrorism or related terms.

Titles of the projects range from "Semiochemical Management Tactics for Filth Flies in Animal Production" to "A Partnership for Pharmaceutical and Economic Development of Wild Lebanese Plants". Some of the projects are actually aimed at thwarting or investigating agroterrorism. Many others simply mention it as one among many applications of research that the scientists would likely be doing anyway for other reasons. Either way, agroterrorism is 'in' in Washington.

## "Agroterrorism Just Old Fashioned Sabotage"

This past summer, the federally funded National Agricultural Biosecurity Center at Kansas State University prepared a report for the US Department of Justice entitled "Defining Law Enforcement's Role in Protecting American Agriculture Against Agroterrorism". It defined "four categories of potential terrorists", only one of them identifiably foreign, who might spread foot-and-mouth or other diseases among cattle, causing billions in economic losses but no human illness:

1. International terrorists

2. Economic opportunists

3. Domestic terrorists (either a Timothy McVeigh type or a "disgruntled employee")

4. Militant animal rights activists (The report notes that "militant elements, such as the Animal Liberation Front, could view an attack on the animal food industry as a positive event.")

It seems that agroterrorism is just a new name for old-fashioned sabotage.

## Report Suspicious Activity?!

Out here in the red states, we often worry that the average American has little knowledge or interest in agriculture. But we need to change our attitude, according to the "Agro-Guard" program sponsored by the NABC and Kansas Bureau of Investigation. Its brochure urges citizens to report to the authorities anyone showing an interest in agricultural matters who has "no logical reason or purpose" for such interest. It exhorts rural Americans to "report any activity around facilities that YOU deem suspicious or out-of-place."

So now I suppose we do things this way:

New Jersey traveler: "Say, do you guys give tours?"

Slaughterhouse manager: "May I see your papers, please? . . . Hey, Merle, call the sheriff!"

In Kansas City each spring, the FBI and federal Joint Terrorism Task Force convene an International Symposium on Agroterrorism. Relying on some of the concepts discussed at the 2005 Symposium and other oft-mentioned scenarios, I composed [a] list of . . . potential threats.

## Food Supply Already Contaminated

Then I realized that much of the damage agroterrorism is expected to cause is already a reality.

Agroterrorists might sicken or kill thousands of Americans by contaminating the food supply with biological agents.

Thousands of Americans? The federal Centers for Disease Control and Prevention (CDC) estimates that "76 million

Americans get sick, more than 300,000 are hospitalized, and 5,000 people die from foodborne illnesses each year."

The flow of food contaminated with nasty microorganisms coming from an evermore-industrialized countryside is heavy and constant. Of the 10 organisms listed by the US Public Health Service as the most serious threats, 7 are carried by meat and dairy products.

In promoting the agroterrorism threat, Senator Collins conjured up a bucolic image: "the fields and pastures of America's farmland." But the overcrowded, filthy conditions of gigantic feedlots and animal-confinement facilities that produce most of our meat are well-known, as are the opportunities for contamination in high-throughput, lightly inspected slaughterhouses.

Cattle consuming a grain-based diet in feedlots (and that's the vast majority of beef cattle in this country) are more likely to have the deadly bacterium E. coli 0157:H7 in their feces than are grass- or hay-fed cattle, and meat is frequently contaminated with feces as it leaves the slaughterhouse.

## Poisoned Water Commonplace Already

What if someone were to poison the rural water supply?

Someone's already doing it. A 1998 CDC report showed that 15% of domestic wells in Illinois, 21% in Iowa, and 24% in Kansas were contaminated with nitrates above a safe level. Most of the nitrates get into wells by escaping the roots of heavily fertilized crops and leaching into groundwater. Consumption of nitrates is associated with methemoglobenemia ("blue baby syndrome") in infants. Many, but not all, studies have shown links between nitrates and various cancers in adults.

A 2004 report by the Kansas Department of Health and Environment surveyed 19,500 miles of rivers and streams in the state. More than half of those miles—10,800—were "impaired for one or more uses" by pollution. Of more than

## Why No Attacks?

If it is so easy to pull off an attack and if terrorists are so demonically competent, why have they not done it? Why have they not been sniping at people in shopping centers, collapsing tunnels, poisoning the food supply, cutting electrical lines, derailing trains, blowing up oil pipelines, causing massive traffic jams, or exploiting the countless other vulnerabilities that, according to security experts, could so easily be exploited?

One reasonable explanation is that almost no terrorists exist in the United States and few have the means or the inclination to strike from abroad. But this explanation is rarely offered.

John Mueller, "*Is There Still a Terrorist Threat?*
*The Myth of the Omnipresent Enemy,*" Foreign Affairs, *October 2006.*

180,000 acres of lakes, 75% were similarly polluted. More than 40% of stream mileage and lake acreage was unable to "fully support" aquatic life, and 69% of lake acreage could not fully support domestic water uses.

In the Kansas study, agriculture was by far the biggest cause of damage to surface waters—exceeding industry, municipal discharge, sewage, urban runoff, mining, and oil drilling combined.

## Antibiotic-Resistant Bacteria

Terrorists might breed bacteria resistant to most or all antibiotics, spreading hard-to-cure diseases among animals and humans.

But they'd be too late. According to a study published this year by CDC scientists, bacterial resistance to multiple antibiotics in human patients comes chiefly from feeding antibiotics to livestock. The bacteria that survive and contaminate the meat of such animals are likely to be resistant.

And, the study showed, resistant bacteria are more likely to cause bloodstream infections requiring hospitalization. A 2004 study found that an outbreak of antibiotic-resistant urinary tract infections of women in California was caused by meat-borne bacteria from antibiotic-treated animals.

In this country, antibiotics are widely fed to livestock even when they aren't sick, because the drugs promote weight gain and profits. That practice has been banned in Europe because it accelerates the development of hard-to-kill bacterial strains.

Vast acreages of crops could be wiped out by inoculation with plant diseases.

Mother Nature is already busy inoculating crops with a massive array of fungi, bacteria, viruses, and insects—some beneficial and some harmful. Over the past 30 years, Kansas wheat production has been reduced by an average 30 to 40 million bushels per year by a dozen different fungal and viral diseases—and that doesn't count insects and mites.

The disease organisms are natural, but epidemics are not; they result when vast acreages are sown to one or a few crop species (e.g., corn and soybeans in the Upper Midwest, wheat in the Great Plains), the fields are kept as free as possible of any other flora or fauna, and only a handful of genetically similar crop varieties are grown.

As late as the 1960s, the United States bioweapons program worked on "weaponizing" two crop diseases, wheat stem rust and rice blast, and the Soviets worked on such pathogens for another couple of decades after that, but neither seems to have come up with an effective way to wipe out a nation's crop entirely.

Remember, the 9/11 terrorists showed an interest in flying crop dusters!

Yes, and I remember editor Alexander Cockburn writing in the print edition of *CounterPunch* that the grounding of all crop dusters for a few weeks was probably one of the few post-9/11 government actions that actually protected citizen's health and lives.

## Pesticides Rampant

Of the 1.2 billion pounds of pesticides (fungicides, insecticides, herbicides, and others) used in the United States, 75% are used in agriculture, and that proportion has been fairly constant over the past 20 years.

The consequences? The following is reproduced from a report by the Natural Resources Defense Council:

Children living in farming areas or whose parents work in agriculture are exposed to pesticides to a greater degree, and from more sources than other children.

The outdoor herbicide atrazine was detected inside all the houses of Iowa farm families sampled in a small study during the application season, and in only 4 percent of 362 non-farm homes.

Neurotoxic organophosphate pesticides have been detected on the hands of farm children at levels that could result in exposures above U.S. EPA designated "safe" levels.

Metabolites of organophosphate pesticides used only in agriculture were detectable in the urine of two out of every three children of agricultural workers and in four out of every ten children who simply live in an agricultural region.

On farms, children as young as 10 can work legally, and younger children frequently work illegally or accompany their parents to the fields due to economic necessity and a lack of child care options. These practices can result in acute poisonings and deaths.

By far the most comprehensive epidemiological study of the effects of ag chemicals is the National Institutes of Health / EPA Agricultural Health Study, which has been running since 1993. Scientists have been monitoring the health of private and commercial pesticide applicators and spouses—almost 90,000 of them so far. The still-unfinished research is suggesting that some ag chemicals present risks to humans. "Outcomes of concern" include cancer, neurologic diseases, reproductive problems, and nonmalignant respiratory diseases.

Meanwhile, the EPA, at industry's urging, continues to permit dosing of human subjects with pesticides in order to test their effects.

A highly trained agroterrorist might infect crops with a toxin-producing fungus and contaminate our food that way.

No terrorists or training necessary. Vomitoxin, produced by the "scab" fungus Fusarium graminearum, and aflatoxin, produced by Aspergillus flavis, have been inflicting enormous headaches and costs on farmers and the grain industry for years. Vomitoxin makes a wheat or barley crop unusable as human food and drastically reduces or destroys its value as livestock feed. Aflatoxin, found most often in peanuts or corn, is carcinogenic.

In the state North Dakota alone, scab has cost farmers $162 million this year and $1.5 billion since 1993. It caused a disastrous epidemic in the southeastern United States in 2003.

Two factors have converged in recent years to make scab much more severe: (a) farmers concerned about soil erosion have reduced or eliminated tillage in many fields, leaving infected crop residue on the soil surface, and (b) grain agriculture in the US continues to emphasize continuous monocultures or unsustainable rotations such as wheat following corn.

## What Terrorism Threats?!

Those who are sounding the agroterrorism alarm acknowledge that the increasing concentration of US agriculture, and its increasingly industrial infrastructure, make it more vulnerable. But those same, homegrown forces are already having consequences that are not easy to distinguish from the results of a hypothetical agroterror attack.

With an agriculture like this, who needs terrorists?

| "Agricultural disease agents intentionally spread amongst crops or livestock in the U.S. have the potential to cause billions of dollars of damage to the U.S. economy."

# Agroterrorism Poses a Significant Economic Threat to U.S. Agriculture

*Rocco Casagrande*

*In the following viewpoint, Rocco Casagrande, testifying before a United States Congressional Committee on Homeland Security, contends that a bioterrorist attack on the nation's agricultural sector would severely cripple the U.S. economy. Casagrande says that the technological barriers to an agricultural attack are easily surmounted and the economic devastation that can be brought about by "agroterrorism" fulfills the goals of many terrorists groups. Rocco Casagrande, a former United Nations weapons inspector in Iraq, holds a PhD in experimental biology and has published numerous articles on biological warfare.*

Rocco Casagrande, "Evaluating the Threat of Agroterrorism," Hearing Before the Subcommittee on Intelligence, Information Sharing, and Terrorism Risk Assessment of the Committee on Homeland Security United States House of Representatives, May 25, 2005. Available at http://frwebgate.access.gpo.gov/cgi-bin/getdoc.cgi?dbname=109_house_hearings&docid=f:23605.wais.

As you read, consider the following questions:

1. What kinds of pathogens are most dangerous to U.S. agriculture, according to Casagrande?

2. Name the six diseases that Casagrande says "could be used that have all the qualities" favorable for an agricultural attack and are endemic to the developing world?

3. How would criminals profit from an attack on agriculture, according to Casagrande?

The threat to US agriculture is primarily economic. Agricultural disease agents, intentionally spread amongst crops or livestock in the US, have the potential to cause billions of dollars of damage to the US economy. These losses will be incurred from disease control costs and associated reductions in tourism, food processing, transportation and trade.

It is my opinion that US agriculture is threatened by a wide variety of actors, from states in economic competition with the US, to fringe animal rights groups, to lone criminals to Al-Qa'ida. The variety of the threat of an attack on the US agricultural system is born out of two main factors: 1) the technological barriers to an attack are easily surmountable by even technically unsophisticated actors, and 2) an attack on agriculture would help fulfill the goals of many state and non-state actors.

Let me begin by commenting on the on the first factor: that the technological barriers to an attack are easily surmountable. Influencing this factor is the nature of the disease agents, the pathogens, that may be used in an attack on agriculture. The pathogens that are most dangerous to US agriculture are those contagious agents that can spread explosively in a herd or between farms. The fact that these pathogens are highly contagious eliminates the need of the adversary to manufacture a complicated device to expose hundreds or thousands of animals or plants to the pathogen during the attack. No weaponization of the pathogen, and the complicated equipment required for that process, is necessary. The simple direct exposure of animals or plants to infected material (such as a tainted cloth dropped into an animal pen or handfuls of infected plant material thrown into fields) may begin an outbreak that affects thousands to millions of animals or acres of crops.

Further facilitating the use of agricultural pathogens is the fact that they are easily handled by even technically unsophisticated actors. First of all, the most contagious agents do not cause significant disease in humans. The fact that an adversary does not need to protect themselves from their agent of choice obviates the need for specialized protective equipment and facilitates manipulation of the agent in rudimentary facilities such as basements or farms. Furthermore, these pathogens are relatively hearty; many can survive in isolated tissues from a plant or animal or on cloth for weeks. No special storage conditions are required during smuggling of the agent into the US. Lack of a requirement for special storage conditions suggests that the agent could be smuggled in easily concealable or disguised containers, such as wine bottles, Tupperware or, for those agents that survive on cloth, impregnated in the clothing of the adversary. Once smuggled into the country, enough agent can be manufactured for an attack by the intentional infection of bins of plant cuttings or captive animals. These living factories could produce kilograms of infected material that could then be introduced into fields or pens all over the US.

The nature of the pathogens that could be used on agriculture, therefore, eliminates the need for sophisticated laboratory equipment for the acquisition, production, processing or dissemination of the agent. Unfortunately, pathogens of this kind are not particularly rare. Foot and mouth disease, Rinderpest, Newcastle disease, African swine fever, wheat smut and rice blast are just a few of the diseases that could be used that have all of the qualities described above. These pathogens are endemic to the developing world and an adversary need only find disease outbreaks to find a source of their agent.

It is not only the nature of dangerous agricultural pathogens, but also the nature of the modern agricultural system that facilitates an attack. Modern US agriculture is vast, mobile and consolidated. Its vastness implies that large feedlots and farms are almost impossible to physically secure, enabling even incautious actors to gain access to their targets. The livestock industry is mobile; animals are moved between states to various facilities that wean, fatten and finish them. This movement enables infected animals to come into contact with thousands of others in facilities across the country. Also, the US agricultural industry is highly consolidated; an attack that affects even one processor would affect a significant portion of the industry.

US agriculture is dominated by big businesses that employ tens of thousands of Americans. The shares of these businesses, the commodities they produce and the futures derived from them, comprise a significant portion of our financial markets. Because of the economic hardship that a disease outbreak can bring, even minor outbreaks or rumors of outbreaks can create shockwaves within stock and futures markets, causing the overnight loss of billions of dollars in market value.

When an outbreak is identified, the system to control and eradicate the disease leads to further economic losses. Exports are halted to prevent the spread to our trading partners. Although our experts are halted, the demand for the commodity does not diminish, and importing nations will seek out other suppliers for goods the US can no longer supply. Once the importers establish a relationship with a new supplier, the US may find it difficult to recapture the lost markets; therefore, economic losses can persist for many years after the outbreak is stamped out. To prevent the spread of the disease within the country, agricultural movement is halted and transportation in agricultural areas may be disrupted. These movement restrictions will affect the transportation and tourism industries and may cause farmers unaffected by the disease to slaughter their animals due to the inability to obtain fodder. When an outbreak is identified on a farm, the diseased animals and all animals at risk of infection (usually all those in the affected premises) are slaughtered. Oftentimes, those animals at risk of infection reside at a different farm near a facility where an infected animal was found; these animals are often killed to create disease firebreaks.

Taken together, these qualities of US agriculture imply that even an attack on a few animals or plants can be spread to a significant portion of the industry quickly due to the nature of the industry. Even if the disease does not spread far, our disease control efforts will magnify the cost of the disease far beyond the cost of the plants or animals directly affected. Further, even outbreaks that are rapidly identified and controlled can cause losses due to market fluctuations.

When these qualities of US agriculture are considered along with the qualities of agricultural pathogens, a grim picture of the technical barriers to an attack comes into focus. Because agricultural pathogens are relatively easy to find, acquire, manipulate and use to strike thousands of animals or plants, adversaries with little technical skill can attempt an attack. Because of control efforts, movement restrictions, and market forces, even an attack that only reaches a single farm may inflict damage beyond its proportions. For these reasons, an attack on agriculture is within the reach of almost any state or sub-state group, or even an individual.

Because technical factors only widen the field of actors who can threaten agriculture, let me turn your attention to the second factor influencing the threat—an attack on agriculture is consistent with the goals of several groups—by addressing the motivation of several types of adversaries in turn.

## An Attack Would Have Huge Impact

A major agroterrorist attack would have substantial economic repercussions, especially when allied industries and services—suppliers, transporters, distributors, and restaurant chains—are taken into account. The fiscal downstream effect of a deliberate act of sabotage would be multidimensional, reverberating through other sectors of the economy and ultimately impacting the consumer.

*RAND Corporation National Defense Research Brief,*
*"Agroterrorism," 2004.*

Rival states have a significant financial motivation to attack US agriculture. By initiating a disease outbreak in the US, rival states could capture our export markets, causing a shift of billions of dollars a year from the US. States prosecuting a shadow war with the US may wish to harm us economically even if they do not directly benefit. The motivation to execute such an attack is underpinned by the uncertainty that an attack will be distinguishable from a natural disease outbreak. What would differentiate the accidental importation of FMD-infected swine from China to Taiwan from the intentional infection of swine shipped to Taiwan? Furthermore, the ambiguity of the US response to an attack on our agriculture may embolden a state adversary. A terrorist attack that kills Americans will surely invite military retaliation. However, would the President risk the lives of soldiers if a rival nation simply caused the destruction of our corn or cows?

For radical ecological and animal rights groups, an attack on agriculture is a means and an ends. These groups loathe the treatment of animals in the US farming system or the fact that a significant portion of US crops are genetically modified. To these groups, an attack on agriculture is not a means to

[sow] economic hardship or to gain profit, but to destroy the industry that offends them. These groups, and their less radical allies, have issued statements wishing for the introduction of devastating disease into the US. The lack of human deaths in an agricultural attack is consistent with these groups somewhat non-violent operations.

Criminals, who wish to profit from an attack on agriculture, are another type of actor who may threaten US agriculture. As. stated above, significant losses can be inflicted due to market changes when a disease outbreak is discovered. Similarly, money can be made through the manipulation of futures markets or selling-short of the stocks of affected companies. Furthermore, the threat of an attack can be used to blackmail agricultural interest groups and large companies. These criminals could be acting alone (due to the facility of the execution of an agricultural attack) or could be in a large group, such as a company wishing to cripple a rival.

Lastly, terrorists bent on destroying the US could use an attack on agriculture as part of a larger campaign. Groups like Al-Qa'ida could seek an agricultural attack as a simple means to undercut one of our greatest economic strengths.

All of these groups have the means to attack agriculture and each group has goals that would be at satisfied such an attack, even if that attack fails to spread to a significant portion of the targeted sector due to the economic costs that even minor outbreaks can cause. For many of these groups, such as countries jockeying for economic advantage and radical ecological and animal-rights groups, no other type of attack can satisfy their goals. To address this threat, new policies and regulations that eliminate the ambiguity in the US response to an attack on agriculture and that reduce our adversaries' potential benefit from such an attack are needed.

I do not mean to imply that an attack on agriculture is imminent. The factors influencing the threat to agriculture have been in place for several decades and yet no large attack has been executed. It is possible that sub-state groups use only weapons that are close at hand and are unlikely to travel to exotic locations to acquire their agent. It is possible that the spread of a plant or animal disease pales in comparison to the theater caused by car bombs or other, more conventional and common types of attacks.

What can be said with some certainty is that, although an attack on agriculture may never come, natural agricultural disease outbreaks strike the US with some frequency. Most measures that can be taken to reduce the damage of an attack on agriculture will likely help in natural disease outbreaks that have happened before and will happen again. Investments in animal tracking systems and disease control assets will surely deliver a concrete benefit even if an attack never materializes.

The threat to agriculture stems from two main factors: the technological barriers to an attack are easily surmountable by the least technically sophisticated groups and an attack on agriculture serves the stated goals of state and non-state actors. Groups that have the motives and the means to attack agriculture include states in economic rivalry with the US, foreign terrorist groups, criminals and domestic groups on the fringe of animal rights and ecological issues, tempering this threat assessment is that, although the vulnerability of agriculture has existed for several decades and groups that have the motives and means to exploit this vulnerability have existed for an equally long time, no large attack on agriculture has occurred in the US or elsewhere. However, steps that can be taken to prevent and attack or mitigate its damage will also benefit the US economy when an inevitable natural disease outbreak strikes our country.

> *"It is difficult to imagine how all food supplies could be affected or even how the total supply of any basic food source could be affected for a significant amount of time."*

# The Economic Impact of Agroterrorism Would Probably Be Small

*Richard D. Farmer*

*The economic consequences to the nation of an agroterrorism attack would probably be small, says Richard Farmer, writing for the United States Congressional Budget Office (CBO). Farmer discusses the range of potential losses and costs from agroterrorism. There are some instances where Farmer says costs could be high, such as if the pathogens or contaminants used are unfamiliar to government officials. However, Farmer thinks the agricultural industry would be able to respond to disruptions and readjust to keep economic losses relatively small in the event of a terrorist attack. Richard Farmer, from the CBO, prepared this paper at the request of the Ranking Member of the House Select Committee on Homeland Security.*

Richard D. Farmer, "Homeland Security and the Private Sector," United States Congressional Budget Office, December 2004. Available at www.cbo.gov/ftpdoc.cfm?index=6042&type=0.

As you read, consider the following questions:

1. What two deadly pathogens do the U.S. Food and Drug Administration consider to be the greatest dangers, according to Farmer?

2. Name two pathogens that Farmer says the United States Department of Agriculture (USDA) routinely tests many meat products for. Name two substances that the USDA does not routinely test for.

3. What famous food and drug tampering case led to requirements for tamper-resistant packaging?

Reports of terrorist groups' interests, as well as the history of events involving food contamination and the use of biological agents, support concerns about the prospect of terrorist attacks on the food and agriculture industry. The industry would be vulnerable to attack because of the large numbers of food items and the many points of access. However, many of those vulnerabilities are already addressed through extensive regulation put in place before September 11 in response to the nation's continuing concerns about food safety. That regulation and the organization of the nation's public health system would help limit the losses from any attacks on food supplies involving a range of known agents. The greatest concern would be threats that could escape or exceed the nation's current detection capabilities or for which an effective response would require an increased level of coordination among agencies and different levels of government.

## Agricultural Vulnerability

The use of natural agents in attacks on agriculture or directly on people is commonly described as bioterrorism. That term would include biological attacks—such as with Bacillus anthracis (anthrax) and smallpox—that might not involve farms and food but would require some of the same protective measures and emergency responses. The security of drugs and drinking water supplies is a particularly important, related concern. And although the main focus of attention in the event of a biological attack would be on the immediate safety of the food supply, much of the value of the industry's output is in areas such as forest products, fibers, and other products that are not related to food—and those nonfood resources could be threatened as well.

## Types of Attacks

The food and agriculture industry is vulnerable to four types of assaults:

- Contamination of food with natural biological agents, such as Clostridium botulism toxin (botulism) and Escherichia coli bacteria (E. coli);

- Contamination of food with man-made contaminants, such as poisonous minerals or chemicals and foreign objects;

- Attacks to disrupt food supplies, including the use of fires, floods, or biological agents such as foot-and-mouth disease or insects; and

- Use of agricultural resources as weapons for attacks on other targets, such as wildfires that spread to residential areas, nitrate fertilizer for use in explosives, pesticides for poisoning, crop dusters to spread toxins, or radioactive materials used in food irradiation.

The Food and Drug Administration (FDA) has identified several specific hazards to the safety of food supplies. Among the biological hazards, the deadly pathogens anthrax and botulism are considered the greatest dangers. Next are salmonella, pathogenic strains of E. coli, and ricin. Among the man-made contaminants that present a threat, the FDA has noted concerns about heavy metals (such as lead and mercury), pesticides, dioxins, and other substances that could be introduced into the food supply.

# Range of Losses

The vulnerability to extensive losses would be relatively small if a disease or contaminant maliciously introduced into the food supply was one with which the industry had experience. The government tests for the most common diseases and requires that outbreaks of many diseases (whether in plants and animals or in the human population) be reported. As a result, it is likely that an attack would be detected early, traced to its source, treated, and contained.

Losses could be significantly higher if the attacks involve substances that can enter the supply chain at a point before or after which their origins cannot be traced, substances that are not tested for, and pathogens or contaminants with which government inspectors or health professionals have little experience. Tests may not be available to detect certain agents within foods, and people's exposure to such substances may not be recognized or reported to appropriate state or national organizations to discern a pattern of assault or initiate a response. Further, detection of and response to new modes of attack may require an increased level of coordination among different federal agencies and between different levels of government.

For example, the Department of Agriculture (USDA) tests many meat products for E. coli and salmonella, but it does not routinely test food supplies for contamination from anthrax or ricin. Records are kept on animals, poultry, and eggs that enable the USDA to trace the source of contaminants back through much of the supply chain. But after meats are delivered to meat processing centers, for example, there is no way to distinguish what herds (or animals from specific regions or countries) went into what batches of meat products for subsequent delivery to stores. The Food and Drug Administration also requires random testing of many food products (in processing and packing facilities and in transit) for certain contaminants. However, for food products, the FDA currently requires only that lot numbers (for tracking purposes) be placed on infant formula and low-acid canned food.

## Terrorists' Intent and Past Incidents

Terrorist groups reportedly have shown interest in exploiting weaknesses in the nation's food and agriculture industry, although little information on that threat is publicly available. The al Qaeda terrorist group is known to have considered using crop duster aircraft, apparently with the intent of distributing toxins or pathogens over crops and populated areas. Members of a related group were arrested in London for trying to manufacture the deadly poison ricin—a product of castor beans.

The number of publicly documented crimes intended to harm people or disrupt supplies is small. However, many of those assaults confirm the potential for serious health and economic consequences. For example, efforts by a religious cult in Oregon to contaminate local salad bars with salmonella in 1984 affected 750 people. Other incidents of food sabotage are more commonly perpetrated by disgruntled employees and affect only a few people. But the consequences can be more widespread than the direct numbers harmed, as illustrated in the 1982 case of cyanide-tainted Tylenol capsules. The immediate effect was seven deaths, but the resulting publicity caused a near-total collapse in national demand for that product and led to at least five imitation attacks in subsequent years, all involving fatalities.

## Potential Costs of Agroterrorism

The immediate consequences of a terrorist attack on food and agriculture may be illness or the loss of life, depending on the nature of the attack and how quickly it is detected. With the important exception of several foodborne outbreaks affecting many thousands, the numbers of people seriously harmed by individual incidents (whether by accident or intent) have been small, at least in part because of current regulations and the success of the nation's public health system in containing outbreaks and limiting losses. As a result, the costs of a terrorist attack may be related more to business losses than human losses. Much of the economic cost would result from the increased costs of replacing lost supplies. That cost might be small for the nation but could differ among regional economies.

Past incidents involving accidental contaminations of the food supply indicate the potential health consequences of an attack and underscore the importance of current food safety regulations and public health institutions. Researchers at the Centers for Disease Control and Prevention estimate that 76 million illnesses, 325,000 hospitalizations, and 5,000 deaths occur every year because of contaminated food. Specific incidents point to how widespread a contamination can become if not detected quickly. About 170,000 people were sickened by salmonella typhimurium in milk from a U.S. dairy plant, and 224,000 people were sickened by salmonella enteritidis linked to ice cream.

Economic costs associated with those threats to health and safety can be significant. For example, USDA estimates that the annual cost to the nation—in terms of medical costs, productivity losses, and costs of premature deaths—from five major foodborne pathogens totals $6.9 billion.

## Economic Consequences Probably Small

Retail sales by food and beverage stores (including groceries) were more than $505 billion in 2003, and agricultural exports were valued at more than $59 billion. However, those types of aggregate measures of the value of annual sales or output are likely to overstate the potential economic cost to the nation of disrupting the industry. It is difficult to imagine how all food supplies could be affected or even how the total supply of any basic food source could be affected for a significant amount of

# Supporting a Resilient Economy

The following options could be helpful to support a resilient economy that is better prepared to deal with an [Foot and Mouth Disease] FMD attack:

• Increase the number of testing facilities

• Analyze whether vaccination as a preventive measure is an effective strategy

• Improve channels for disseminating information to avoid mass panic and enforce proper quarantine restrictions

• Explore better compensation programs to assist those affected, particularly in the non-farming sectors

• Explore ways to improve loan programs and unemployment benefits for those directly affected by the attack

*ICF Consulting, "Perspectives,"*
ICF International, *Summer 2003. Available at*
*www.icfi.com/Markets/Homeland-Security/doc_files/costs_terrorist.pdf.*

time. Replacement supplies (from storage or from unaffected regions) and very close substitutes (from the perspective of consumer welfare) are readily available for virtually every type of food product. People could draw on current inventories of the targeted item (in home and stores), stop consuming any particular food item altogether, stay away from food from a particular agricultural region, or not frequent a given grocery chain or fast-food outlet. For the nation as a whole, the sales lost by products or establishments that were directly affected by an attack would be made up in increased sales elsewhere.

The cost to the national economy would, for the most part, be the increase in the cost of supplying those replacements or substitutes (and the loss in consumer satisfaction). For a number of reasons, even that residual cost should be small. First, the food and agriculture industry is well adapted to the prospect of disruptions from weather and occasional health incidents. For example, in anticipation of periodic crop losses, the most vulnerable crops are often grown in multiple regions, and individual farmers diversify their plantings and purchase crop insurance. Similarly, food distributors and grocers already have experience with identifying and recalling contaminated lots. Second, government programs are in place to ensure food safety (and limit the health consequences of an attack) and to sustain the income of some agricultural producers (and, indirectly, the businesses and regions that depend on them). As a result, the economic effects of a terrorist incident might well fall within the realm of industry experience and current public plans for detection and response.

## Cases Where Costs Could Be High

Circumstances could exist, however, in which the cost of replacement would be high or the cost to society would be greater than the immediate loss associated with any replacement or substitution for lost supplies. For example, replacement costs could be greater than otherwise if there was a high market concentration in the targeted food or agriculture industry. Where only one or a few businesses account for a large share of sales, the opportunities for drawing on inventories or switching to other suppliers may be limited. Also, in some cases of contamination, the costs of replacing lost supplies may entail more than simply ramping up production. For some diseases, there may be few options to eliminate the risk of further contamination other than burning facilities, plants, and livestock.

The cost to society would be greater than the direct losses associated with replacement and substitution if there were noneconomic losses to consider. For example, if the attack resulted in a major forest fire, costs could include the loss of recreational benefits, erosion from damaged watersheds, and loss of wildlife—values that can be difficult to express in dollar terms. And attacks involving pesticides or other toxins could cause environmental damage.

Regardless of the economic cost to the nation, the potential loss for the particular producers or regional economies could be significant. For example, in seven states, farm employment accounts for more than 5 percent of the total state work force. The nature of many agricultural commodities is that they are produced in discrete growing seasons: once the current supply is lost, the domestic market has to wait through a new cycle.

## Consumer Concerns and Long-Term Effects

Broad consumer concerns about the safety of food supplies can have other adverse economic effects. Any public demonstration of vulnerability to attack can lead to costly, long-term (if not permanent) changes in product handling and consumer demand. The Tylenol case, for instance, led to requirements for tamper-resistant packaging. The situation with mad cow disease, although not deriving from terrorism, has led to new costs, too—from having to discard certain animal parts, restrict the contents of animal feed, and inspect slaughtered animals. Based on the costs to beef producers in Japan for inspecting slaughtered animals, that requirement alone could entail $1.2 billion in expenses for the much larger U.S. beef industry if applied here. (Japan spends $40.9 million a year inspecting only about 1.3 million slaughtered cattle. The United States slaughters about 37 million cattle annually.)

# Periodical Bibliography

*The following articles have been selected to supplement the diverse views presented in the chapter.*

| | |
|---|---|
| Jeffrey M. Bale, Anjali Bhattacharjee, Eric Croddy, and Richard Pilch | "Ricin Is a Biological Weapon," *Center for Nonproliferation Studies*. February, 20, 2004. |
| Greg Blonder | "Bracing for Bioterror," *Business Week Online*. May 22, 2007. |
| Christoper F. Chyba and Alex L. Greninger | "Biotechnology and Bioterrorism: Unprecedented World," *Survival. The International Institute for Strategic Studies*. Summer, 2004. |
| John Mintz | "Technical Hurdles Separate Terrorists From Biowarfare," *Washington Post*. December 30, 2004. |
| Jim Monke | "Agroterrorism: Threats and Preparedness," *CRS Report for Congress*. August 25, 2006. |
| Oliver Morton | "Biology's New Forbidden Fruit," *New York Times*. February 11, 2005. |
| John Mueller | "Is There Still a Terrorist Threat?: The Myth of the Omnipresent Enemy," *Foreign Affairs*. September/October 2006. |
| Liise-anne Pirofski and Arturo Casadevall | "The Weapon Potential of a Microbe," *Trends in Microbiology*. June, 2004. |
| Lawrence M. Wein and Yifan Liu | "Analyzing a Bioterror Attack on the Food Supply: The Case of Botulinum Toxin in Milk," *Proceedings of the National Academy of Sciences*. July 12, 2005. |
| Mark Williams | "The Knowledge," *Technology Review*. March 2006. |
| David Willman | "Selling the Threat of Bioterrorism," *Los Angeles Times*. July 1, 2007. |

OPPOSING
VIEWPOINTS®
SERIES

CHAPTER 2

# What Are the Issues Associated with Biodefense Research?

# Chapter Preface

During World War II, in a northeast province of China, in the city of Pingfang, at a place called Unit 731, the Japanese Imperial Army conducted some of the most horrific experiments known to humankind. Unit 731 was one of many covert biological warfare research facilities of the Imperial Japanese Army where scientists studied the feasibility of biological warfare. At Unit 731, Chinese, Korean, Russian, European, and American test subjects, culled from local villages and prisoner-of-war camps, were deliberately infected with the pathogens causing cholera, bubonic plague, anthrax, and hemorrhagic fever. As they began to exhibit symptoms of disease, they were taken to "treatment rooms," tied to operating tables, and dissected alive. As they screamed in agony, their bodies were cut open, and their organs were removed so scientists could see the effects of the diseases on their internal organs. The Japanese scientists did not use anesthesia because they didn't want to distort the scientific results. In other gruesome experiments, test subjects had their limbs frozen until the tissue died and became gangrenous in order to study the effects of frostbite. In survivor testimonials, it was revealed that these horrifying experiments were conducted on men, women, children, and even infants.

In addition to Japan, several other countries conducted biological weapons research during World War II, although no other country tested their biological weapons on humans—using animals instead. Most countries initiated their programs based on fears that potential enemies might be developing biological weapons. Great Britain set up its program and convinced the United States to assist them, based on fears that the country was going to be the target of German biological bombs. In 1942, United States president Franklin Roosevelt said, "I have been loath to believe that any nation, even our present enemies, would be willing to loose upon mankind such terrible and inhumane weapons." But Secretary of War Henry Stimson convinced Roosevelt that other countries were developing these weapons and that the United States should too. "Biological warfare is . . . dirty business," he wrote to Roosevelt, "but . . . I think we must be prepared." The U.S. Biological weapons program officially began in the spring of 1943. The center of the U.S. program was at Camp Detrick in Maryland. The British had asked the United States to help them research the use of two bacteria to use as biological weapons: The bacterium *Bacillus anthracis*, which causes anthrax disease, and the bacterium *Clostridium botulinum*, which produces one of the most lethal toxins known to man.

All told, the United States, Britain, Canada, France, Germany, Italy, Japan, and the Soviet Union conducted research on the use of pathogenic microbes as weapons of war during World War II. However, Japan was the only country that actually deployed biological weapons during the war. They bombed several Chinese villages with fleas carrying the bubonic plague.

When the war ended, America dispatched investigators to Germany and Japan to investigate the extent of their bioweapons technology. The United States did not find an extensive program in Germany. Surprisingly, Hitler himself had given the order not to develop offensive biological weapons. However, in Japan, the United States found Unit 731.

The United States was interested in the scientific data obtained at Unit 731 and wanted to keep it out of the hands of the Soviets. The Japanese research at Unit 731 had gone far beyond anything that other countries had even considered. The Japanese had shown that biological agents could be effectively deployed against humans and cause massive casualties. In his book, *Biohazard*, Ken Alibek, a former Soviet bioweapons researcher writes, "Like us, Americans learned about Japan's germ warfare operations from captured documents and prisoners of war . . . Their reports convinced Washington that biological weapons could be developed in greater quantities and with far greater effectiveness than anyone had suspected."

In the autumn of 1945, General Douglas MacArthur granted immunity from war crimes prosecution to members of Unit 731 in exchange for research data on biological warfare. MacArthur was worried that the Soviets would get hold of Unit 731 data if war crime tribunals were conducted. "The value to the U.S. of Japanese biological weapons data is of such importance to national security as to far outweigh the value accruing from war crimes' prosecution," said MacArthur. The scientists at Unit 731 were never held accountable for the atrocities that occurred there, unlike Nazi scientists who were prosecuted as war criminals.

Most countries, except the United States and the Soviet Union, ended their biological weapons programs shortly after World War II. The German and Japanese programs ended with their defeat in the war. Canada, France, and the United Kingdom ended their programs in the 1950s. But the United States and the Soviet Union continued their research for several more years, carrying out a biological arms race as each country wanted to have the "supreme" biological weapon. The United States maintained a biological research program until 1969, while the Soviets conducted bioweapons research until about 1992.

Shortly after the United States gave up its bioweapons program, the international community adopted an agreement—the Biological and Toxin Weapons Convention (BWC)—to ban the development and stockpiling of biological weapons. Under the BWC, countries agree not to acquire, develop, possess, produce, or stockpile biological weapons. Countries are allowed to maintain biological substances that can be justified for "prophylactic," protective, or other peaceful measures, such as developing vaccines or medicines to combat diseases. But they cannot maintain these things for hostile measures.

The United States no longer has an "offensive" biological weapons program, but it still conducts "biodefensive" research into vaccines and medicines that can protect against bioweapons. Some scientists believe the United States should conduct more of this research, while others believe it is unsafe and unethical. These and other viewpoints about biodefense research are presented in the following chapter.

> *"It is imperative that we move ahead with a biodefense agenda as rapidly as possible. To do otherwise would be extremely risky and, in many respects, unconscionable."*

# The United States Should Pursue Biodefense Research

### *Rona Hirschberg, John La Montagne, and Anthony S. Fauci*

*In the following viewpoint, Rona Hirschberg, John La Montagne, and Anthony Fauci contend that biodefense research is crucial. They claim that the events of September 11, 2001, and the anthrax attacks occurring later that year revealed the nation's vulnerability to a bioterrorist attack. Developing medical countermeasures, such as vaccines and antidotes to smallpox, anthrax, and other biological weapons is necessary to prepare and protect the nation against bioterrorism and falls within the statutorily required tasks of the National Institute of Allergy and Infectious Disesases (NIAID). Anthony Fauci is the director of the NIAID; Rona Hirschberg is a senior program officer at the agency; and John La Montagne was the deputy director until his death in November 2004.*

Rona Hirschberg, John La Montagne, and Anthony S. Fauci, "Biomedical Research—An Integral Component of National Security," *The New England Journal of Medicine*, vol. 350, May 20, 2004. Copyright © 2004 Massachusetts Medical Society. All rights reserved. Reproduced by permission.

As you read, consider the following questions:

1. What are three resurging infectious diseases that the authors mention in the viewpoint?

2. The authors note that important progress has been made in the development of vaccines against which three biological agents?

3. What program is essential to the success of the biodefense research agenda and includes funding for biosafety level 3 and 4 facilities.

The attacks on the World Trade Center and the Pentagon on September 11, 2001, and the deliberate release of anthrax spores that occurred soon thereafter starkly revealed our vulnerability to the threat and reality of multiple categories of terrorism, including biologic, chemical, nuclear, and radiologic assaults. As a result of the events of late 2001, the focus on national security in the United States has intensified greatly, and extensive efforts to prepare for and prevent future attacks have been undertaken, particularly by the newly established Department of Homeland Security. In the arena of biologic terrorism against the civilian population, the Department of Health and Human Services has taken a lead role; efforts have focused on surveillance and activities to promote public health preparedness, led by the Centers for Disease Control and Prevention (CDC), and biomedical research, led by the National Institutes of Health (NIH), particularly the National Institute of Allergy and Infectious Diseases (NIAID).

## National Institute of Allergy and Infectious Diseases (NIAID)

The NIAID supports a broad-based program of basic and applied research to prevent, diagnose, and treat infectious and immune-mediated diseases. Integral to this mission is the responsibility to conduct biomedical research aimed at addressing the constant threat of naturally occurring, newly emerging, and reemerging or resurging infectious diseases. The specific mandate of the NIAID in the post–September 11 national security effort is to support research that will ultimately lead to the development of medical countermeasures in the form of therapies, vaccines, and diagnostic tools to protect the country from deliberate attacks with biologic agents. This role is consistent with the NIAID's long-established mandate with regard to infectious diseases, including emerging diseases such as AIDS and the severe acute respiratory syndrome (SARS) and resurging infectious diseases such as malaria, West Nile virus, and tuberculosis. Although the factors that precipitate the appearance of emerging, resurging, and deliberately propagated infectious diseases are quite distinct, the development of countermeasures for all three may be addressed with very similar scientific approaches.

## Biodefense Research Strategic Plan

Many members of the research communities in microbiology, infectious diseases, and immunology responded to the events of 2001 by expressing their willingness to contribute their skills and insights to the evolving biodefense efforts. The NIAID harnessed this spirit through a series of blue-ribbon panel meetings that were designed to enlist the best and the brightest in the development of a research agenda and strategic plan for biodefense research. The outcome of these discussions and deliberations is found in the *NIAID Strategic Plan for Biodefense Research* and the more detailed research agendas for agents in CDC categories A, B, and C, which are those pathogens most likely to be used and to cause harm in a bioterrorist attack. These documents provide the framework for addressing the research and training needs posed by this challenge to national security.

These plans are living documents that are regularly updated as progress is made. In August 2003, a progress report for category A agents was published and made available online. As detailed in the report, 50 new and expanded initiatives have been implemented, and substantial scientific accomplishments have been achieved in a relatively short period. Specifically, important progress has been made in the development of new or improved vaccines against anthrax, smallpox, and Ebola virus; the capacity for testing drugs and vaccines in animals, particularly nonhuman primates, has been markedly expanded; promising new drugs for the treatment of smallpox are being pursued; the genomes of all category A agents have been sequenced; and our understanding of the basic properties of the agents that pose threats has improved markedly. Despite these accomplishments, we are only in the early stages of a long-term process.

Our biodefense research agenda consists of a variety of programs designed to balance basic, translational, and applied research, with the objective of developing new and improved vaccines, drugs, and diagnostic tests. These programs involve collaboration with the academic community, as well as with the biotechnology sector, large pharmaceutical companies, and government partners. . . .

## Regional Centers of Excellence and Biocontainment Laboratories

Among a variety of new and expanded programs, the Regional Centers of Excellence for Biodefense and Emerging Infectious Diseases Research (RCEs) and the National and Regional Biocontainment Laboratories deserve particular mention. The RCE program has established regional consortia of investigators who operate within a synergistic and coordinated framework. The goals of the program are to develop and conduct programs of investigator-directed research, particularly in the area of agents in CDC categories A, B, and C; train people to conduct research related to biodefense and emerging infectious diseases; develop and maintain comprehensive core facilities that support the research and training activities of the RCE; make these core facilities available to qualified investigators from academia, biotechnology companies, the pharmaceutical industry, and other appropriate entities in the geographic region of the center; develop translational research capacity for the testing and validation of concepts for vaccines, therapies, and diagnostic tools for biodefense and emerging infectious diseases; and provide facilities and scientific support to first-line responders in the event of a national biodefense emergency. The NIAID funded eight RCEs in the fall of 2003.

## Biosafety Level Research

The program for constructing biocontainment laboratories is essential to the success of the biodefense research agenda and includes funding for the design, construction, and certification of biosafety level 4 and biosafety level 3 facilities. The national laboratories will include capacity for research at biosafety levels 4, 3, and 2; facilities for the conduct of research in nonhuman primates and other animals; and facilities and resources for small-scale phase 1 clinical trials in humans. The regional laboratories will provide capacity for research at biosafety levels 3 and 2, as well as facilities for research in animals. The laboratories will provide additional infrastructure for the RCEs and other NIAID-funded biodefense research. They will also be available to assist public health efforts in the event of a bioterrorism emergency. These will be state-of-the-art facilities, designed and built to the highest standards of safety and security, where 21st century research can be conducted. Together with the RCEs, these laboratories will provide a network for linking basic science and discovery to the product-development pathway, creating the capacity to address important scientific problems in a safe and expeditious manner. The NIAID funded two national laboratories and nine regional laboratories in the fall of 2003.

## An Aggressive Research Program Is Needed

Development and deployment of safe, effective medical countermeasures against biological weapons agents of concern remains an urgent priority. The National Institutes of Health (NIH), under the direction of the Department of Health and Human Services, is working with the Department of Homeland Security, the Department of Defense, and other agencies to shape and execute an aggressive research program to develop better medical countermeasures. NIH's work increasingly will reflect the potential for novel or genetically engineered biological weapons agents and possible scenarios that require providing broad-spectrum coverage against a range of possible biological threats to prevent illness even after exposure. Additionally, we have begun construction of new labs. We are striving to assure the nation has the infrastructure required to test and evaluate existing, proposed, or promising countermeasures, assess their safety and effectiveness, expedite their development, and ensure rapid licensure.

*The White House, "Biodefense for the 21st Century,"*
*The White House, April 28, 2004.*
*Available at www.whitehouse.gov/homeland/20040430.html.*

Successful research requires not only access to appropriate technology and facilities, but also a robust corps of talented and committed scientists. Training and other efforts to increase the number of investigators engaged in this effort are essential, and to this end, several training programs in biodefense research have been initiated or expanded.

## Biodefense Research Crucial

Although we all hope that events such as the anthrax attacks of 2001 will never occur again and that our efforts to prepare and protect ourselves will be successful, the challenge of bioterrorism will be with us indefinitely. It is difficult to assess the probability of future deliberate releases of microbes or their products, but the potential consequences of such attacks are enormous. Furthermore, we will certainly face naturally occurring emerging and resurging infectious diseases, and the potential for devastation associated with such diseases as pandemic influenza or SARS may surpass that associated with bioterrorism. The research agenda of the NIAID and the NIH is designed to prepare for and provide protection against both types of threats. Given the nature of these threats, it is imperative that we move ahead with the biodefense research agenda as rapidly as possible. To do otherwise would be extremely risky and, in many respects, unconscionable.

| *"Research at some of these [biodefense] laboratories should be cause for concern to all."*

# Biodefense Research Is Cause for Concern

### Laura H. Kahn

*In the following viewpoint, Laura Kahn expresses concern about the United States' biodefense research activities. Kahn thinks the research being done at national laboratories, such as Lawrence Livermore and Fort Detrick, may be violating the United Nations Biological Weapons Convention, and she is concerned about the effectiveness of the Office of Homeland Security in monitoring the research. She also questions the merits and ethics of research that uses monkeys as models to study the smallpox vaccine. Kahn thinks the public must be better informed. Laura Kahn is a physician and staff member at the Woodrow Wilson School of Public and International Affairs at Princeton University.*

As you read, consider the following questions:

1. According to Kahn, what was the initial mission of the Lawrence Livermore National Laboratory in California?

Laura H. Kahn, "A Dangerous Biodefense Path," *The Bulletin Online*, March 5, 2007. Reproduced by permission of *Bulletin of the Atomic Scientists: The Magazine of Global Security News & Analysis*. Available at www.thebulletin.org/columns/laura-kahn/20070305.html.

2. Why does Kahn say the "animal rule" does not work and may be partly to blame for unethical smallpox research using monkeys?

3. Instead of research using smallpox, Kahn thinks research should be done to make what other vaccine safer?

Is the United States close to violating the Biological and Toxin Weapons Convention (BWC)? At the fifth annual American Society of Microbiology (ASM) Biodefense Conference in Washington, D.C., in February, Bernard C. Courtney, scientific director of the Department of Homeland Security's National Biodefense Analysis & Countermeasures Center, described how the U.S. government is building a network of laboratories to characterize and anticipate future biothreats, as well as conduct biological risk assessments. Research at some of these laboratories should be cause for concern to all.

## Concerns about Laboratories

One of these laboratories is the Lawrence Livermore National Laboratory in California. It will house the new Biological Threat Characterization Center. This is the same laboratory that was just given a federal award to design the nation's first new nuclear weapon in two decades. Livermore has been doing bioscience research since 1963, but its initial mission was to characterize the biological consequences of ionizing radiation. Since then, its research scope has expanded dramatically, and it is now embarking in an area of biological research that was not clearly articulated in Courtney's talk. This vagueness is not new. A 2002 editorial in the *Daily Californian* also expressed concern about the kind of biothreat research Livermore will conduct.

In addition to Livermore, Homeland Security is also building a large National Biological Weapons Analysis Center facility on the U.S. Army Medical Research Institute for Infectious Diseases (USAMRIID) campus at Fort Detrick in Maryland.

Courtney mentioned that this facility will conduct some classified research. Officially, the United States has not done any classified biological research since it terminated its offensive biological weapons program in 1969. However, in their book *Germs, New York Times* reporters Judith Miller, Stephen Engelberg, and William Broad uncovered "biodefense" research conducted by the CIA and Pentagon that arguably pushed the BWC's boundary limits.

## No Confidence in Homeland Security

Now, the United States will be doing classified research under the auspices of Homeland Security. The mission is to provide the nation with the scientific basis for awareness of biological threats and attribution of use against the U.S. public. Courtney assured the audience that the research will not violate the BWC because a "Compliance Review Group" composed of senior Homeland Security officials will oversee the research. The majority of them will be lawyers and scientists.

One could argue that the composition of this committee would not meet muster with any local Institutional Biosafety Committee. Where are the ethicists? What about outside representation? Will the minutes be available under the Freedom of Information Act?

The core issue is whether Homeland Security should be in charge of biodefense research in the first place. It is a new, very large, unwieldy agency that hasn't had a long track record to instill confidence. Created after 9/11, Homeland Security is the third largest cabinet department in the U.S. federal government. Its mission is to prevent and deter terrorist attacks and protect against and respond to threats and hazards to the nation. But one could argue that some of its efforts to accomplish this mission, particularly in the area of biological threat assessment, are as bad as any outside threats. . . .

## Secret Lab

On the grounds of a military base an hour's drive from the capital, the Bush administration is building a massive biodefense laboratory unlike any seen since biological weapons were banned 34 years ago.

The heart of the lab is a cluster of sealed chambers built to contain the world's deadliest bacteria and viruses. There, scientists will spend their days simulating the unthinkable: bioterrorism attacks in the form of lethal anthrax spores rendered as wispy powders that can drift for miles on a summer breeze, or common viruses turned into deadly superbugs that ordinary drugs and vaccines cannot stop.

The work at this new lab, at Fort Detrick, Md., could someday save thousands of lives—or, some fear, create new risks and place the United States in violation of international treaties. In either case, much of what transpires at the National Biodefense Analysis and Countermeasures Center (NBACC) may never be publicly known, because the Bush administration intends to operate the facility largely in secret.

*Joby Warrick, "The Secret Fight Against Bioterror,"*
The Washington Post, *July 30, 2006.*

## Questionable Research

It is important to note, however, that it is not just Homeland Security that's embarking on research of questionable ethics and merit. In a subsequent session at the ASM conference, Peter Jahrling, a researcher at the Integrated Research Facility at the National Institutes of Health/National Institute of Allergy and Infectious Diseases [NIH/NIAID] and a former researcher at USAMRIID, presented his work on developing an animal model for smallpox. This work is not classified and has been profiled in the March 15, 2002 *Science* by Martin Enserink and Richard Stone in an article entitled, "Dead Virus Walking."

In a high containment biosafety level 4 laboratory, Jahrling and his colleagues have been infecting monkeys, specifically cynomolgus macaques, with smallpox via aerosol and/or intravenous routes. The monkeys were resistant to the aerosolized version of the virus but succumbed to high viral titers that were intravenously injected. Jahrling showed graphic pictures of monkeys covered in smallpox pustules. Similar research is also being done at Russia's State Research Center of Virology and Biotechnology. China and other nations are understandably concerned about the U.S. and Russian monopoly on this virus.

The purpose of this research is unclear. Terrorists would likely seek to expose humans by aerosolization, not intravenously. Smallpox was eradicated because there was no animal reservoir. Therefore, no animal model could accurately represent a human infection. So why is this research being done on animals?

## Why Animals?

The Food and Drug Administration's (FDA) "animal rule" is partly to blame. In May 2002, the FDA published "Approval of Biological Products When Human Efficacy Studies Are Not Ethical or Feasible." This rule is known as the animal rule because it amends the new drug and biological product regulations to provide evidence of the efficacy of a new drug against bioterrorism agents on animals as a substitute for human studies. But with a virus such as smallpox, the animal rule doesn't work because smallpox never infected animals in nature.

After two centuries of using the cowpox vaccine—an approach with some dangers—it was efficacious and safe enough to eradicate the disease from human populations. Trying to force smallpox infections into animals is unethical and dangerous; one could argue that it pushes the boundaries of meeting the criteria of one of the experiments of concern in the National Academy of Sciences report by trying to expand the host range of a deadly pathogen. Instead, biodefense research should be done on making the cowpox vaccine safer.

## Where Is Public Debate?

Aside from the questionable utility and ethics of this research, laboratory accidents and inadvertent laboratory-acquired infections do occur even in high containment laboratories. Research on smallpox should simply not be done.

Where is the media in all of this, and where is the public debate? Unfortunately, the U.S. media focuses more attention on Anna Nicole Smith's death than on what the federal government is doing in the name of fighting terrorism. Is this federal research agenda under the Bush administration the biological equivalent of its misadventure in Iraq? As with the misinformation over Iraq and the hype leading up to the war, the media is dropping the ball on this issue. The public must be informed.

> "To take the comparison between bioterrorism and pandemic flu full circle, it must be noted that some have argued that influenza would make an ideal biological weapon."

# Flu Preparedness and Bioterrorism Research Are Similar

*Bioterrorism Watch*

*In the following viewpoint, the newsletter Bioterrorism Watch proposes that bioterrorism and flu preparedness research build upon each other. Bioterrorism Watch editors note that many of the same health care issues are raised regardless of whether health care workers are responding to a bioterrorist attack or a pandemic flu outbreak. The authors point out that the legendary 1918 flu pandemic, the SARS outbreak in 2002 and 2003, and Hurricane Katrina provide lessons for both flu preparedness and bioterrorism preparedness. Bioterrorism Watch provides up-to-date bioterrorism preparedness information to nurses and other health-care workers.*

Kathleen Gensheimer, Martin Meltzer, Alicia Postema, and Raymond Strikas, "The Fire Next Time: Pandemic Flu, Bioterrorism, and Ghost of SARS," *Bioterrorism Watch Newsletter*, March 1, 2007. Copyright © 2007 AHC Media LLC. Reproduced by permission.

As you read, consider the following questions:

1. According to the authors, the federal government recently decided to classify future pandemics based on what?
2. According to the authors, racial and class distinctions became an issue in the 2001 anthrax attacks when questions arose about the perceived differences between the protections given to what two groups of people?
3. What is Tamiflu?

The massive national effort to meet the threat of pandemic influenza the last few years has generally better prepared public health and the medical system against bioterrorism, experts note.

The possibility that avian influenza A (H5N1) may mutate into a strain easily transmissible between humans has forced the health care system to look at critical issues like surge capacity, infection control measures, educating staff, allaying fears and dealing with shortages of critical equipment such as mechanical ventilators.

"People have had to do a lot of work preparing for a pandemic and that will serve bioterrorism preparedness as well," says Eric Toner, MD, senior associate at the Center for Biosecurity at the University of Pittsburgh Medical Center (UPMC). "The issues raised for pandemic flu with regards to protecting health care workers with additional protective equipment [e.g., N95 respirators] would be applicable to some bioterrorist agents that are contagious such as smallpox, viral hemorrhagic fevers, or pneumonic plague."

## Preparedness Overlap

In addition, there is some overlap with regard to the need to cohort [classify or group] patients and enforce respiratory etiquette at the triage level. "All of those infection control measures would apply to any respiratory contagious illness, whether flu or bioterrorism," he says. "In addition, all of the issues related to surge capacity—at least surge capacity within the walls of the hospital—apply."

Regardless of the agent and its origin, tough questions remain about how to expand the number of hospital beds, ensure adequate staff to provide care and accumulate the necessary stockpiles of medication and supplies.

"These issues all overlap," Toner says. "The difference is that we would expect in most bioterrorism scenarios the whole country would not be affected at one time. With a pandemic, we do expect that more or less the whole country will be affected simultaneously. It makes some of the surge capacity issues a little bit different, but nonetheless there is a lot of similarity."

Indeed, even the most dire bioterrorism scenarios usually envision some initial local event, holding out the hope of containment in a city or area that is presumably already suspected to be on the prime target list for terrorists. But even a pedestrian seasonal flu virus—let alone a pandemic bug for which there is likely to be no direct vaccine match initially—can appear in disparate regions with near simultaneity. That means even the least desired target on our bioterrorists' list is about as likely to face pandemic flu as the next locale. If all are vulnerable, all must be ready. Therein lies the problem.

"Hospitals have done a lot of work in preparing for a pandemic, but there is an awful lot yet to be done," Toner says. "Some of the problems are insufficient funding and just that hospitals are overwhelmed on a day-to-day basis just managing a flood of patients with meager resources. Some of it has been that there hasn't been sufficient guidance that's really practical at the ground level. Progress is being made at a pretty good rate, but if a severe pandemic were to hit it would still be catastrophic."

## Some Places "Pre-Disastered"

True enough no doubt but some places will be much more prepared than others for an unusual reason. They have—to borrow the term made famous by the novel *The World According to Garp*—been "pre-disastered." What group of hospitals, for example, is more prepared to deal with pandemic flu than those in Toronto? The hard lessons learned there have been shared with all in the stinging final report on severe acute respiratory syndrome (SARS), but clinicians and public health workers there have been through a fierce trial that no drill can simulate. Game speed—not practice speed—the coaches call it.

"Any time professionals and decision makers go through an actual emergency, they are gaining real-life experience that can be redeployed in a new situation that they hadn't envisioned in the first place," says Monica Schoch-Spana, PHD, senior associate at the Center for Biosecurity at UPMC.

Thus, whether designed by man or formed in nature, the current calamity informs the next. "[In 2001,] there was a major fire in a train tunnel in the city of Baltimore," she says by way of example. "That crisis brought together public health, emergency management, and the mayor and his staff in a way that equipped them much better to deal with the [subsequent] anthrax letter attacks. So it's building up those trusting relationships, getting more experience communicating with a concerned public and the media that are directly transferable across different extreme events."

A medical anthropologist, Schoch-Spana notes that it was no coincidence the federal government recently decided to use hurricane rankings to classify future pandemics. "The decision by federal health officials to characterize pandemic flu in terms of severity like a hurricane is driven by historical events," she says. "Americans, even those who don't live in hurricane-prone regions, came to understand just how strong an effect a hurricane could have through Katrina. I think that they were

## Similarities Include Large Number of Casualties

In the list of potential bioterrorist agents, influenza would be classified as a category C agent. While previous influenza pandemics were naturally occurring events, an influenza pandemic could be started with an intentional release of a deliberately altered influenza strain. Even if a deliberately altered strain is not released, an influenza pandemic originating from natural origins will inevitably occur and will likely cause substantial illness, death, social disruption, and widespread panic. Globally, the 1918 pandemic killed at least 20 million people. This figure is approximately double the number killed on the battlefields of Europe during World War I. In the United States alone, the next pandemic could cause an estimated 89,000–207,000 deaths, 314,000–734,000 hospitalizations, 18–42 million outpatient visits, and 20–47 million additional illnesses. These predictions equal or surpass many published casualty estimates for a bioterrorism event. In addition to the potential for a large number of casualties, a bioterrorism incident and an influenza pandemic have similarities that allow public health planners to simultaneously plan and prepare for both types of emergencies.

*Kathleen Gensheimer, Martin Meltzer, Alicia Postema and
Raymond Strikas, "Influenza Pandemic Preparedness,"
Emerging Infectious Diseases, December, 2003.*

trying to find a way to define the range of possibilities to an American public most of whom have not lived through even a moderate pandemic flu. They seized on a familiar metaphor."

## Lessons from 1918

To take the comparison between bioterrorism and pandemic flu full circle, it must be noted that some have argued that influenza would make an ideal biological weapon. This concern became less theoretical last year, when researchers successfully reassembled the legendary 1918 influenza viral genome and published the results for consideration by friend and foe alike. Among those questioning the wisdom of that decision was Kenneth Alibek, MD, PhD, DSc, former chief scientist and deputy director of bioweapons research in the former Soviet Union. Now in the department of molecular and microbiology at the National Center for Biodefense at George Mason University in Washington, DC, Alibek says the Soviets were always interested in weaponizing 1918 flu. It has been argued that influenza would not make a good bioweapon since it could not be controlled once released, and even if you developed a vaccine the weaponized virus still would be subject to ongoing mutation. Nevertheless, Alibek says the sheer virulence and transmissibility of the 1918 strain make it attractive as a bioweapon.

Still, influenza is not likely at the top of anyone's list of bioterrorism concerns, particularly since it a seasonal killer that we face annually with a striking complacency. In any case, preparing for a pandemic flu essentially takes the origin question out of the equation, Schoch-Spana adds. "Conversations about influenza mostly turn on it being a naturally occurring outbreak, simply because pandemic flu is a regular occurrence," she says. "The origin doesn't really matter; it's the management challenges that are extreme if it is a novel strain. Pandemic flu is a great example of an extreme public health emergency. There are certain scenarios that could involve release of a biological agent among civilians that could create a similar effect."

In a published analysis applying the historical lessons of the 1918 pandemic to bioterrorism, Schoch-Spana argues that it is critical to characterize the outbreak accurately and promptly. In 1918, poor disease reporting systems seriously hampered the ability of public health officials to keep the public informed and to manage the outbreak. Influenza was not a reportable condition before the outbreak, and no well-developed system existed through which federal, state, and local health entities could sketch the course of the disease, she found.

"The question of whether things are getting worse or better is a constant for everyone, including the professionals who are trying to control the crisis and the people who are living through it," she says. "The more capacity that we have to describe the crisis as it is unfolding, resolving or fully ending the better."

Another lesson from 1918 is to earn public confidence in emergency measures, preferably before an event occurs. In the 1918 pandemic, some community members embraced public health measures to control flu, but others resisted orders seen as inconsistent, burdensome, or contrary to common sense or deeply held values, she found.

"Whether you are talking about an act of bioterrorism, pandemic flu or any other large-scale outbreak of infectious disease, you will always get a higher degree of collaboration, understanding, and even forgiveness for how things turn out if there has been more upfront interaction with the public," she says. "Starting pre-event makes a great deal of sense. Apart from mass communications, you also want to be reaching out to civil society institutions—communities of faith, professional societies of all kinds, trade unions—all of the different organizations that people belong to in their local and work communities. Include those institutions in emergency planning, [outlining] what will be required of the government and what will be required of community groups."

## Guarding Against Social Disparities

In the aftermath of Hurricane Katrina, another lesson from 1918 seems particularly apt: Guard against discrimination and allocate resources fairly. Though there were many displays of sacrifice and courage, the 1918 pandemic also "pitted groups against one another in an effort to assign blame or to protect access to limited resources. Rumors circulated in the United States that German spies, some disguised as doctors and nurses, were spreading flu and that Bayer aspirin, a German product, was infected with flu germs," Schoch-Spana found.

Racial and class distinctions became an issue in the 2001 anthrax attacks, when questions arose about the perceived discrepancies in the measures taken to protect postal workers vs. U.S. senators. "We are now living in a post-Katrina context as well," she says. "These kind of large scale crises don't happen in a vacuum. We have longstanding concerns regarding health disparities in the United States. Past events really do shape people's levels of trust in the folks in charge of managing the crisis. I don't think nationally we have adequately publicly addressed these issues of disparity with regard to Katrina. I think that is going to be hanging over the heads of politicians and emergency managers in a pandemic flu context or any other [emergency]."

## Sharing Antivirals and Vaccines

The social disparity issue—the "haves" and the "have-nots" if you will—could play out in another context with pandemic flu. Though some national supplies will be available, federal planners have essentially left it to individual states to stockpile antivirals such as Tamiflu. Such drugs could lessen the severity of infections and protect key groups such as health care workers in the absence of a vaccine. Yet states have been left to their own devices—and budgets—in deciding how much of the drug they should stockpile. As a result, during a pandemic some states will be more adequately supplied than others.

"Some people have said that all of the stockpiles of Tamiflu ought to be national," Toner says. "That gets away from the states having to make the in-the-field decisions. I think there is merit to that argument but that is not the way it was set up.

Right now, there is a relatively modest national stockpile, but the states have to pitch in and do their part. It's not just with stockpiling antivirals, it is also trying to organize their hospitals. Some states are quite proactive, others are coming along quite reluctantly. States that haven't prepared are going to be bad places to live and to be hospitalized in when a pandemic happens."

The situation is somewhat reminiscent of the Atlantic Storm bioterrorism exercise in 2005, which showed that world leaders with limited smallpox vaccine would be reluctant to share it after an attack ensued.

"I don't expect governors will share their state stockpiles [of Tamiflu]," Toner says. "I don't think it will happen. If a state has not stockpiled, they are going to be in trouble."

*"The rapid buildup of new laboratories, personnel, and funding for biodefense could have a significant downside for other important areas of research."*

# Biodefense Research Has Hurt Other Research Areas

**Barton Reppert**

*In the following viewpoint, Barton Reppert argues that the U.S. government is spending billions of dollars for biodefense research, while other areas of research are suffering. Reppert says top-level scientists are speaking out against the diversion of money from microbial physiology, genetics, and other studies to fund research into what many consider an exaggerated threat. Barton Reppert is a science and technology writer.*

As you read, consider the following questions:

1. According to Reppert, how much more did the federal government spend on civilian biodefense research in 2005 compared to 2001?

2. According to Reppert, how many grants were awarded to study bioweapons agents between 1996 and 2000? How many in 2001?

Barton Reppert, "The Biodefense Buildup: Fallout for Other Research Areas," *Washington Watch*, April 2005. Reproduced by permission.

3. Name two scientists who Reppert says are critical of the "biodefense buildup."

Massive expansion of the US biodefense program since 2001 has yielded fresh career opportunities for thousands of American scientists handling infectious disease work. With the Bush administration determined to develop better countermeasures against bioterrorism, this trend is likely to continue for the next several years.

## Money Pouring into Biodefense Leaves Other Research Hurting

However, the rapid buildup of new laboratories, personnel, and funding for biodefense could have a significant downside for other important areas of research—and, some scientists contend, may actually contribute to the erosion of this country's public health infrastructure.

The fiscal year (FY) 2006 federal budget, sent to Congress on 7 February, signaled President George W. Bush's intention to keep pouring money into biodefense. "We have spent or requested nearly $19.2 billion since September 11, 2001," Secretary of Health and Human Services Mike Leavitt told reporters, "and that investment is showing tangible results."

According to research analyst Ari Schuler at the University of Pittsburgh Center for Biosecurity, in [2005] combined spending for civilian biodefense by seven federal departments and agencies is estimated to total about $7.647 billion—approximately 18 times more than FY 2001 outlays of $414 million.

## Dozens of New Laboratories

One of the results of the steeply ramped-up biodefense effort is a network of new, high-security laboratories for research on infectious diseases. The network, funded by the National Institute of Allergy and Infectious Diseases (NIAID), a part of the

National Institutes of Health (NIH), will comprise two large national biocontainment laboratories (to be built at Boston University's Medical Center and at the University of Texas Medical Branch in Galveston), along with 14 to 17 smaller regional biocontainment laboratories. The two national facilities will include a substantial amount of biosafety level 4 (BSL-4) laboratory space, while the regional facilities will feature [biosafety level-3] BSL-3 and [biosafety level 2] BSL-2 labs. In addition, NIAID is funding the establishment of 10 Regional Centers of Excellence for Biodefense and Emerging Infectious Diseases Research, each of which comprises a consortium of universities and complementary research institutions, to support the NIAID biodefense research agenda.

Proponents of that agenda, including Dr. Anthony Fauci, director of NIAID, argue that biodefense research represents money well spent because it is dual-purpose: it is valuable not only for developing better vaccines, diagnostics, and therapeutics against bioterrorist agents but also for coping with naturally occurring infectious diseases. Several critics within the scientific community, however, contend that the biodefense effort is largely a politically motivated overreaction—following the fall 2001 anthrax-by-mail incidents—to a limited threat.

## Critics Speak Out

One outspoken critic, Richard Ebright, a molecular biologist and professor of chemistry and chemical biology at Rutgers University, has initiated and circulated to colleagues an open letter to Elias Zerhouni, NIH director, charging that the priority placed on biodefense research since 2001 has been accompanied by "a massive efflux of funding, institutions, and investigators from work on non-biodefense-related microbial physiology, genetics, and pathogenesis."

The letter, signed by more than 750 researchers, says the number of grants awarded by NIAID referencing "prioritized bioweapons agents" has increased by 1500 percent, from 33 in

## Lawmakers Want to Know How Money Is Spent

In a rare sign of bipartisanship close to the midterm elections, Senate and House Democrats and Republicans asked federal auditors Monday to examine how the government has spent more than $18 billion on biodefense capabilities and technologies since the Sept. 11, 2001, attacks.

The government began pouring billions of dollars into biodefense research and development after the terrorist attacks and after the deaths of five people exposed to anthrax spores mailed to two Senate offices and news organizations. The mailings remain an unsolved crime.

"Having reached the fifth anniversary of the anthrax attacks, we believe Congress and the administration would benefit from a comprehensive assessment by the Government Accountability Office of currently deployed airborne or environmental biological threat detection technologies and those that are planned or under development," lawmakers wrote in a letter to Comptroller General David Walker.

*Chris Strohm, "Senators Seek Audit of More than $18 Billion in Biodefense Spending," Congress Daily, October 31, 2006.*

1996–2000 to 497 since 2001. By contrast, grants awarded to study non-biodefense-related model microorganisms have decreased by 41 percent over the same period, from 490 down to 289, while grants to study non-biodefense-related pathogenic microorganisms have decreased by 27 percent, from 627 down to 457.

"The diversion of research funds from projects of high public-health importance to projects of high biodefense but low public-health importance represents a misdirection of

NIH priorities and a crisis for NIH-supported microbiological research," declares the scientists' letter, urging that Zerhouni "take corrective action."

## Exagerrated Threat

Another critic of the biodefense buildup, Mark Wheelis, an expert on biological weapons at the University of California at Davis, says he believes that "the threat of a mass-casualty bio-terrorist attack has been greatly overestimated. The possibility of such an attack is clearly not zero, but it's probably quite a bit less likely than many people think." Regarding the new network of biocontainment laboratories, Wheelis observes that "a small increase in our capacity to do work on very serious pathogens under high containment is reasonable. . . . But plastering the country with BSL-3 and BSL-4 labs is going to degrade our public health infrastructure more than it will aid it."

The Bush administration has renewed its resolve to move ahead with a heavily funded fight against the perceived threat of bioterrorism. At the same time, it is clear that the continuing biodefense buildup will not only involve "hot zone" pathogens but also generate a substantial amount of heated debate within the American scientific community.

> *"The reintroduction of the smallpox virus into an unprotected population could cause substantial morbidity and mortality and overwhelm public health resources."*

# Smallpox Poses a Significant Threat to Public Health

### Agency for Healthcare Research and Quality

*In this viewpoint, the United States Agency for Healthcare Research and Quality (AHRQ) asserts that smallpox is a serious public health threat that could cause widespread casualties. The viewpoint provides a summary of presentations made during an audioconference on smallpox. AHRQ scientists believe that terrorists may have been able to get their hands on the smallpox virus, and they discuss ways that local health care workers, i.e. those at the city and state level, can prepare for and respond to a smallpox terrorist incident. The AHRQ is an agency within the United States Department of Health and Human Services whose task is to support research that improves public health, among other things.*

Agency for Healthcare Research and Quality, "Addressing the Smallpox Threat: Issues, Strategies, and Tools. Bioterrorism and Health System Preparedness," *U.S. Department of Health and Human Services*, January, 2004. Available at www.ahrq.gov/news/ulp/btbriefs/btbrief1.htm.

As you read, consider the following questions:

1. When did the last case of smallpox in the United States occur?

2. According to the U.S. Centers for Disease Control and Prevention(CDC), what is the percentage of unvaccinated people expected to die in a smallpox outbreak?

3. According to Edward Gabriel, what is an especially important element of local-state-federal coordination in the event of a public emergency?

A bioterrorist attack using smallpox would pose a significant threat to public health in the United States. The reintroduction of the smallpox virus—which has not infected anyone in the world for nearly three decades—into an unprotected population could cause substantial morbidity and mortality and overwhelm public health resources. While the threat of such an attack is of national concern, it is at the local level that public health officials and health system planners must be ready to respond.

On March 3, 2003, an audioconference sponsored by the Agency for Healthcare Research and Quality (AHRQ) examined the implementation of the Centers for Disease Control and Prevention's (CDC's) smallpox vaccination program and strategies to assist public health officials in responding to a potential smallpox outbreak. . . .

This issue brief . . . identifies tools to help hospital administrators and emergency responders prepare for an outbreak of smallpox and other deadly diseases that can be caused by biological or chemical attacks.

## Smallpox Concerns Reemerge

The last case of smallpox in the United States occurred in 1949. The last natural case documented in the world occurred in Somalia in 1977. In this country, vaccination against smallpox stopped in 1972 and, in 1980, the World Health Organization declared that the disease had been globally eradicated. Although there is no reason to believe that smallpox presents an imminent threat today, the terrorist attacks of September 11, 2001, and the anthrax attacks that followed them have heightened concern that terrorists may have obtained the virus and will attempt to use it against the American public.

## Smallpox Is High-Priority Threat

Smallpox is one of six biological agents that the CDC views as a high-priority threat because of the effects of the disease and its potential for large-scale dispersal. William Raub listed five reasons why smallpox is considered a threat:

> It is highly lethal; without vaccination, 30 percent of those infected can expect to die, and of those who survive there can be lifelong, serious morbidities of various types;

> The disease is readily communicable from person to person; respiratory droplets are sufficient to carry the virus, and therefore ordinary day-to-day contact can be sufficient exposure to spread the disease;

> Few people have effective immunity; with vaccination having ended in the United States in the 1970s, individuals born since that time have no immunity and those of us who were vaccinated earlier have little or none, depending on the length of time involved;

> We have no established treatment; the vaccine itself is protective within a few days of exposure, but once the symptoms present we have no drugs or other means to treat, much less cure, this disease; and

> Enemies of the United States may obtain the variola virus, which causes smallpox.

After eradication of the disease in 1980, only two official stockpiles of variola virus remain—one in the United States

## Staggering Danger

The ease of production and aerosolization of the [smallpox] virus is well documented. Researchers estimate that only 10-100 virus particles are necessary to infect someone. Thus, smallpox is a potential biological weapon of staggering danger.

*Christopher J. Hogan, "Smallpox,"* emedicinehealth.com
*(last reviewed October 31, 2005).*
*Available at www.emedicinehealth.com/smallpox/article_em.htm.*

and the other in the Soviet Union. Much of the former Soviet Union's supply is still not accounted for today. "When scientists and engineers left that country following the breakup of the former Soviet Union, we fear that they left with more than their know-how," said Dr. Raub. "They may indeed have left with samples of the virus." . . .

## Smallpox Threat Requires Coordination Communication

Edward Gabriel, Deputy Commissioner for Preparedness in the New York City Office of Emergency Management, stressed that planning for a smallpox threat—or any public health emergency—must begin with communication and coordination among local emergency authorities. He described incident management planning as "a way to bring everybody to the table and get them to speak the same language." "Everybody" includes not only hospitals and emergency medical services, but also local public health departments and fire, police, and ambulance personnel. In addition to "speaking the same language," incident management planners should get to know one another on a first-name basis, face to face, and should consider each other as part of the same emergency response team.

Local planners should also work with State and Federal representatives. In response to a call-in question, Mr. Gabriel said that one of the lessons of 9/11 was the importance of coordination of emergency management at the local, State, and Federal levels. It is important to know who the contact points are and "where to go for what resources, how to get them, and how your chain works from the lower level to the State level to the Federal level."

An especially important element of that local-State-Federal coordination in the event of any public emergency is communication with the public. "Our experiences from September 11 taught us the importance of projecting one voice and a consistent message to the public," said Gabriel. Nancy Ridley added that one of the highest priorities in making a smallpox plan successful is being prepared to counter "an epidemic of fear" among the public.

## New Tools Help Prepare for Deadly Diseases

If a smallpox outbreak were to occur, a large-scale vaccination program would be necessary. Researchers at Weill Medical College of Cornell University have designed a new computer model to help hospitals and health systems plan antibiotic dispensing and vaccination campaigns to respond to bioterrorism or large-scale natural disease outbreaks. The model was funded by AHRQ and developed by researchers after testing a variety of patient triage and drug-dispensing plans.

Now, for the first time, hospital planners can estimate the number and type of staff needed to vaccinate an entire community in an efficient and timely fashion. For example, the model can quantify the staff required to vaccinate one million people over 14 days. The model can be downloaded to run on common spreadsheet software customized for use by health officials at all levels of government, hospital administration, and emergency medical planning.

"Models like this allow planners to think with numbers when designing mass prophylactic response strategies," said lead model designer Nathaniel Hupert of Weill Medical College. Modeling also forces a critical examination of assumptions about how a large-scale vaccination plan would be executed, particularly the issue of resource availability. Dr. Hupert cautioned that while "models are useful to guide planning, they don't replace the real thing, which is exercises and drills that test the response of a health care system."

> "[The government's vaccination effort]
> is a campaign based on emotion and
> fear rather than facts and science."

# The Smallpox Threat
# Is Exaggerated

*George J. Annas*

*In this viewpoint, George J. Annas argues that the government's effort to have medical personnel vaccinated against smallpox is misguided. Vaccinia (smallpox vaccine) is itself contagious and exposure carries significant risks, including death. Annas believes its use is not justified by the vague fears of bioterrorism that the government has put forward. Professor Annas chairs the department of Health Law, Bioethics, and Human Rights at Boston University and has written widely on these subjects.*

As you read, consider the following question:

1. According to Annas, why are health-care workers resisting the government's effort to have them vaccinated?
2. What are some of the risks of being vaccinated that Annas mentions?

George J. Annas, "Smallpox Vaccine: Not Worth the Risk," *The Hastings Center Report*, Garrison, NY: 2003. Copyright © 2003 Hastings Center. Reproduced by permission.

3. Does Annas believe that the Department of Homeland Security's recommendations on how Americans can protect themselves from a biological attack are useful?

In late February [2003] *Washington Post* reporter Cici Connolly summarized the current state of President Bush's plan to voluntarily vaccinate 500,000 civilian health care workers against smallpox under the headline "Bush Smallpox Innoculation Plan Near Standstill: Medical Professionals Cite Possible Side Effects, Uncertainty of Threat." There are many suggested explanations for the fact that only about 4,000, or less than 1 percent of the projected number, had been vaccinated at the time of this writing. But the headline itself got it right: physicians just don't believe that the benefits of the vaccine are outweighed by its risks. And an objective examination of the elements of informed consent to smallpox vaccine must conclude that the risk-benefit assessment of the vast majority of physicians is correct.

## Vaccination Could Do More Harm than Good

First the benefits. The benefits are secret. Remarkably, and against all tenets of disease control, the CDC [U.S. Centers for Disease Control] refuses to share with the physicians, or anyone else, their estimate of the probability of a smallpox attack, where it might occur, and even who, if anyone, actually possesses the smallpox virus. Instead the CDC asks us all to take its claims about this extraordinarily unlikely occurrence on faith. In the words of CDC Director Julie L. Gerberding (to a U.S. Senate Appropriations Subcommittee on 29 January 2003): "I can't discuss all of the details because some of the information is, of course, classified. But I think our reading of the intelligence that we share with the intelligence community is that there is a real possibility of a smallpox attack from either nations that are likely to be harboring the virus or from individual entities, such as terrorist cells that could have access to the virus. So we know it's not zero. And I think that's really what we can say with absolute certainty that there is not a zero risk of a smallpox attack." This is not only useless information, it is counterproductive. The only known way to prevent a biological attack is to prevent the creation and use of a bioweapon—and this can only be done by a combination of inspections and public disclosure of any activities that might lead to the production of such a weapon. Secrecy makes sense only for the attacker, not the defenders.

On the other side of the ledger are the risks. An Institute of Medicine panel made what I think are sensible general recommendations (the IOM was not asked if it thought the administration's smallpox vaccine policy itself was advisable) to the CDC in a report issued on 16 January 2003: (1) to highlight the unique nature of this vaccination campaign, "focusing on the delivery of clear, consistent, science-based information," (2) to "proceed cautiously," (3) to "use a wide range of methods of proactive communication . . . to reach diverse audiences," including the general public, and (4) to "designate one credible, trusted scientist as key national spokesperson for the campaign . . ." (www.nap.edu/catalog/10601.html). To date, the last recommendation has been explicitly rejected, and the other three don't seem to have been taken very seriously. In terms of the risks of the vaccine itself, physicians continue to be referred to a CDC website that hasn't been updated since August 2002, even though smallpox vaccine reactions in both military and civilian recipients have been reported in the press. A quick cruise through the side effects of the smallpox vaccine illustrated on the site is not reassuring. For example, if vaccinia [The cowpox virus. Controlled exposure to vaccinia provides protection against smallpox.] gets in your eyes you can develop vaccinia keratitis, which may result in loss of sight. The frequency of this risk is "unknown" (www.bt.edc.gov/training/smallopoxvaccine/reactions/default .htm).

## Smallpox: More Bark than Bite

In 1972 Thomas Mack concluded in his review of post-1949 smallpox in Europe that "under contemporary conditions smallpox cannot be said to live up to its reputation. Far from being a quick-footed menace, it has appeared as a plodding nuisance with more bark than bite." Why, then, is smallpox currently regarded as a credible biological weapon and why are governments making contingency plans for its possible use? One reason is that its bad reputation persists.

*Hugh Pennington, "Smallpox and Bioterrorism,"*
Bulletin of the World Health Organization, *2003.*

Physicians are even more worried about the possibility of transmitting a vaccinia infection to their immunocompromised patients [sick patients with weak immune systems] and their family members. Hospitals are worried about staffing (understaffed emergency departments could contribute to more deaths than an actual smallpox attack), and everyone is worried about the financial consequences of a major side effect, including death. Their confidence is not bolstered when they realize that no plans are yet in place to provide compensation for injury, and that no federal money has been allocated for compensation.

## The Government's Case for Vaccination Is Unconvincing

The CDC's pronouncements have not inspired trust. Nor was February a good month for homeland security in general. The Secretary of Homeland Security, for example, raised our alert status to orange, and we were encouraged to "prepare" by buying duct tape and plastic sheeting. The chance of either of these being helpful in a bioterrorist attack is zero (unless you could personally capture the terrorist and wrap him up in duct tape). Nor are many Americans comforted by Department of Homeland Security's new website, Ready.gov. Here's the Department's advice on how to "protect yourself" from a biological attack: "If you become aware of an unusual and suspicious release of an unknown substance nearby . . . quickly get away. Cover your mouth and nose with layers of fabric that can filter the air but still allow breathing. . . . Wash with soap and water and contact authorities."

So we are left with an unknown risk (greater than zero) that unknown people or countries will launch an attack whose effects can be reduced with a vaccine that itself has known serious risks and costs, both to the recipients and others, and which is being offered by federal officials who use "national security" excuses, vague color codes, and almost comical self-protection suggestions to persuade us to follow their advice. In short, it is a campaign based on emotion and fear rather than facts and science. A public opinion poll published in the *New England Journal of Medicine* in late January showed that regarding smallpox, most Americans would follow the lead and advice of their physicians if asked by the president to take the smallpox vaccine. American physicians seem to have spoken: given what we now know, the benefit is not worth the risk.

# Periodical Bibliography

*The following articles have been selected to supplement the diverse views presented in this chapter.*

| | |
|---|---|
| Pete Alfano | "As Biodefense Research Booms, Reward Is Weighed Against Risk," *Fort Worth Star-Telegram*. August 28, 2007. |
| Mitzi Baker | "Scientists Take Smallpox Research into the Molecular Age," *Stanford Report*. October 6, 2004. |
| Matthew E. Berger | "Firms Find Biodefense Too Risky a Business," *CQ Weekly*. April 23, 2007. |
| Christopher F. Chyba | "Biotechnology and the Challenge to Arms Control," *Arms Control Today*. October, 2006. |
| Paul Dvorak | "Biodefense: The Best Defense After a Biological Attack May Be a Good Filter," *Medical Design*. December, 2006. |
| Gigi Kwik Gronvall, Joe Fitzgerald, Allison Chamberlain, Thomas V. Inglesby, Tara O'Toole | "High-Containment Biodefense Research Laboratories: Meeting Report and Center Recommendations," *Biosecurity and Bioterrorism: Biodefense Strategy, Practice, and Science*. 2007. |
| Trevor Findlay | "Verification and the BWC: Last Gasp or Signs of Life?" *Arms Control Today*. September, 2006. |
| Stephen C. Harrison, et al. | "Discovery of Antivirals Against Smallpox," *Proceedings of the National Academy of Sciences*. August 3, 2004. |
| Christopher Hudson | "Doctors of Depravity," *Daily Mail*. March 3, 2007. |
| Lim Li Ching | "Smallpox Should be History," *CommonDreams .org*. April 7, 2005. |
| MSNBC | "Destruction of Smallpox Virus Delayed Again," *MSNBC News Services*. May 18, 2007. |

OPPOSING
VIEWPOINTS®
SERIES

CHAPTER 3

# How Should the United States Prepare for and Protect Against Bioterrorism?

# Chapter Preface

The smallpox virus causes pus-filled lesions to erupt in the mouth and nose and on the hands, feet, body, and face of its victims. When the lesions erupt, the skin separates from its underlying layers, causing excruciating pain. The victim usually dies two weeks later. The initial symptoms of inhalation anthrax disease may resemble a common cold. After several days, the symptoms usually progress to severe breathing problems, shock, swelling of the tissues surrounding the brain and spinal cord, and death. Symptoms of the plague include fever, coughing up blood, abdominal pain, and diarrhea. Patients usually die from two-to-six days after exposure. According to the U.S. Centers for Disease Control and Prevention (CDC), smallpox, anthrax, and plague are three of the most likely biological agents to be used in a bioterrorist attack.

There are thousands of pathogenic (i.e. disease-causing) microbes in nature, but the smallpox virus, the anthrax bacterium, and the microbe that causes plague have certain characteristics that make them particularly effective biological weapons. They are rugged, meaning they can survive in many different environmental conditions, and they are easily dispersed. They incubate inside their host for relatively long periods of time before causing initial symptoms, which are non-specific (i.e. resembling the cold or flu) and easily misdiagnosed. Thus, those infected can work, go to school, and travel all the while spreading the infection. Finally, they have a 30-to-50 percent mortality rate, meaning 30-to-50 percent of those infected will die. Scientists and military experts believe that smallpox, anthrax, and the plague are a bioterrorist's weapons of choice.

The variola virus, which causes smallpox, is considered the number one bioterrorist threat because of its fatality rate and transmissibility. Smallpox is an ancient disease that has wiped out hundreds of millions of people around the world. It is similar to the common chicken pox disease in that it causes pus-filled blisters to erupt on infected individuals. However, smallpox is far deadlier. In the 20th century alone, the disease is responsible for killing some 300–500 million people. Smallpox is very contagious, and it has a relatively long incubation period before initial symptoms occur. This means that an event can occur in which large numbers of people are exposed, and they can pass the virus on to others in diverse geographical locations. Therefore, the disease can become widespread very quickly. Smallpox is considered the most likely biological agent to be used in bioterrorism.

*Bacillus anthrasis*, the bacterium that produces anthrax disease, is a good candidate as a biological weapon for several reasons. Anthrax is one of the oldest recorded diseases of sheep and cattle and is believed to be the sixth plague mentioned in the book of Exodus in the Bible. *Bacillus anthrasis* produces inactive spores that can be dried and powdered, are easy to work with, and are readily dispersible in the air. Anthrax can cause infections of the lung, skin, and digestive tract. The respiratory form is the most dangerous. When the spores are inhaled, the warm, moist conditions of the respiratory tract cause them to reactivate, and they begin multiplying. Initial symptoms include chest pain and breathing difficulty. As the bacteria proliferate, they enter the blood stream and release a lethal toxin that causes tissue destruction, bleeding, and death. The U.S. military considers anthrax a major biological weapons threat and has a mandatory anthrax vaccination policy to protect service men and women against the disease.

*Yersinia pestis*, which causes plague, is a potential biological threat because it is easy to cultivate and is highly infectious. The plague is responsible for one of the deadliest pandemics in human history, the Black Death of the 14th century where an estimated 75 million people were killed. Symptoms of pneumonic plague, caused by respiratory infection with *Yersinia pestis*, include fever, coughing up blood, abdominal pain, and diarrhea. Patients usually die from two-to-six days after exposure. *Yersinia pestis* normally infects rats and other rodents. Humans most often get the plague when they are bitten by a rat flea carrying the disease. During World War II, the Japanese Army created numerous plague epidemics when they dropped bombs laden with plague-infected rat fleas on northern Chinese cities.

Most experts agree with the CDC that smallpox, anthrax, and the plague are among the most likely biological agents to be used in a bioterrorist incident. However, there is a lack of consensus about the best way to prevent or prepare for attacks using these or other biological agents. The authors of the viewpoints in the following chapter offer their opinions on this important topic.

"As a result of the more than $3 billion investment Congress and the Administration devoted [since 2001], the frontlines of public health are better prepared to detect terrorism and deal with its consequences."

# Bioterrorism Preparedness Programs Are Necessary to Protect Public Health

*Charles A. Schable*

*In this viewpoint, Charles Schable, who is testifying in front of a U.S. Congressional Committee, discusses how the Centers for Disease Control and Prevention (CDC) is working to prepare for a bioterrorist attack. Among Schable's key points is that early detection is crucial for responding to and containing a bioterrorist threat. Charles Schable is the director of the U.S. Bioterrorism Preparedness and Response Program.*

Charles A. Schable, "Centers for Disease Control and Prevention (CDC) Bioterrorism Preparedness Efforts: Protecting Public Health," *Testimony Before the Committee on Science, United States House of Representatives*, May 3, 2004. Available at www.hhs.gov/asl/testify/t040503.html.

As you read, consider the following questions:

1. According to Schable, how many states can transmit information among state and local public health officials, hospitals, emergency departments, and law enforcement?

2. According to Schable, national disease detection can best be described as what?

3. Name one example of how states are using their bioterrorism funding, according to Schable.

CDC [the U.S. Centers for Disease Control and Prevention] continues to make vast strides toward achieving optimal terrorism preparedness and emergency response capacity at the federal, state and local levels and is committed to strengthening the capacity of the public health system to respond to both routine and emergent health threats. To achieve this imperative, we must continue to prepare the broader public health infrastructure to respond to a wide range of public health emergencies. I will address how CDC works with state and local governments to prepare for a bioterrorist attack, explain some of the systems and tools used by CDC to detect and respond to a bioterrorist attack and describe CDC's role in response and coordination with other state and local health officials, and other health service providers.

## Getting States and Cities Prepared

As a result of the more than $3 billion investment Congress and the Administration devoted since 2001, the frontlines of public health are better prepared to detect terrorism and deal with its consequences, and there are specific initiatives underway at CDC and in each state to make America safer.

While much progress has been made strengthening the nation's defenses against biological attacks, President Bush instructed his administration to review its efforts and find new and better ways to secure America. The result of this review is

Biodefense for the 21st Century, a recently approved presidential directive that builds on our past accomplishments, specifies roles and responsibilities, and integrates the programs and efforts of various communities—national security, public health, law enforcement, etc.—into a sustained and focused national effort.

States and localities have made substantial progress toward achieving optimal levels of preparedness since the terrorist attacks of fall 2001. For example, every state has developed an emergency preparedness and response plan and nearly 90 percent of states have trained public health practitioners in responding to terrorism. In addition, every state either has achieved or is moving toward around-the-clock capacity to send and receive critical health information, and 42 states can transmit information among state and local public health officials, hospitals, emergency departments, and law enforcement. CDC's overarching goal in this arena is to have systems in place in each community that protect citizens from infectious diseases, environmental threats, and terrorism, and these achievements represent substantial progress toward that end. . . .

## CDC's Role in Response and Preparedness

In the event of a bioterrorist attack in the United States, CDC would provide public health advice to and support the Department of Health and Human Services in orchestrating the public health response to the attack. CDC would confirm that a biological agent had been released, identify the agent, determine how the agent was or is transmitted, and provide guidance in the development and implementation of effective control measures. CDC would assist the state and local health agencies in addition to the efforts described above, by providing federal resources in support of critical health and medical efforts, to include medical material housed within the Strategic National Stockpile; deploying public health subject matter experts and technicians to assist in managing efforts necessary to detect possible additional bioterrorist attacks; and providing recommendations on immunization and prophylaxis of the at risk population and guidance and recommendations for the treatment, isolation or quarantine of infected individuals. CDC would provide recommendations related to occupational safety issues for first responders and work on risk communication issues related to public health.

## Detecting Disease Early

An important element to successful defense against any threat to the nation's public health, whether naturally occurring or deliberately caused, continues to be accurate, early recognition of the problem.

Disease surveillance systems can prepare the nation for potential terrorist threats. "Disease surveillance systems" or disease detection systems, address one important aspect of our nation's overall public health preparedness. CDC, in collaboration with our federal, state, and local partners is working to build systems that can: (1) rapidly detect an event in our communities; (2) mobilize the appropriate response to contain the event, and (3) ensure affected communities quickly return to a sense of normalcy. These are what we refer to as our foundations of public health readiness.

National disease detection can best be described as the ongoing collection, analysis and dissemination of public health data related to illness and injury. These ongoing data collection and analysis activities enable public health officials to detect disease early, thus resulting in faster intervention to control and contain the consequences created by the causative agents. Without these early detection systems, the consequences of outbreaks of infectious disease and human exposures to agents such as chemicals and radiation would take a much greater toll by way of increased illness, injury, and in some cases death. Recent events, such as the SARS, monkeypox and avian influenza outbreaks, have underscored the essential role early detection systems play in mobilizing rapid response. Detection of a disease almost always occurs at the local level where health care professionals encounter patients seeking medical assessment or treatment. A clinician's ability to quickly recognize and identify symptoms of unusual illnesses on the frontline has been critical to the CDC's ability to recognize unfolding disease events and implement containment measures to prevent further spread of disease, thus mitigating further harm to the public.

Awareness and diagnosis of a condition by a clinician or laboratory is a key element of our current disease detection systems. Clinicians and laboratories report diseases to state and local health departments, which in turn share information with CDC. CDC works with its public health partners to define conditions that should be reported nationally. Health departments share these definitions and guidelines with health care providers, infection control practitioners, emergency department physicians, laboratorians, and other members of the health care system to ensure accurate and timely reporting.

Many local reporters of disease incidence still report to public health authorities on paper via facsimile. If a case of illness is particularly unusual or severe (such as a case of anthrax), the local health care worker may call the local health department immediately to report the case. Current reporting systems are largely paper-based and burdensome to both providers and health departments, often resulting in reports which are neither complete nor timely. In addition to initial detection, these detection and reporting systems play a pivotal role in the detection of subsequent cases and help support the management of the event once a response/investigation are initiated. Such information is vital to coordinating response decisions, which ultimately lead to the containment of an outbreak.

## Improving Detection Infrastructure

A comprehensive detection reporting system requires a strong foundation at all levels of local, state, and federal public health agencies. CDC has been working with state and local health agencies for many years to build the public health infrastructure to improve disease detection and reporting systems.

Some examples of how states use their bioterrorism funding include:

- Initiating implementation of a secure web-based disease detection and reporting system to improve the timeliness and accuracy of disease reporting.

- Implementing a new hospital tracking system to detect possible outbreaks by monitoring the number of patient admissions and ambulance diversions at hospitals. This system provides a way for hospitals to obtain instant messages and alerts.

- Developing early warning systems based on symptom data from emergency departments to detect unusual patterns of illness and automatically alert hospitals and public health agencies when the incidence of disease exceeds a critical threshold. Use of such early warning systems might enable the earliest possible response and intervention before an outbreak or epidemic spreads.

Other related activities useful for early detection of emerging infections or other critical biological agents include CDC's Emerging Infections Programs (EIP). Through the EIP, state and local health departments receive funds to conduct population-based surveillance that goes beyond their routine function to develop "next generation" surveillance science, and often involves partnerships among public health agencies and academic medical centers. In addition, CDC has established networks of clinicians that serve as "early warning systems" for public health by providing information about unusual cases encountered in the clinical practices. As noted earlier, these relationships, particularly between health care providers and local health departments, are the foundation on which disease detection systems operate.

## Public Health Information Network

For many years CDC has made significant achievements in building or enabling state and local health agencies to build information systems that support the practice of public health. However, many of these systems operate in isolation, not capitalizing on the potential for a cross-fertilization of data exchange. A crosscutting and unifying framework is needed to better integrate these data streams for early detection of public health issues and emergencies. The Public Health Information Network (PHIN) provides this framework. Through defined data, vocabulary standards and strong collaborative relationships, the PHIN will enable consistent collection and exchange of response, health, and disease tracking data among public health partners. Ensuring the security of this information is critical as is the ability of the network to work reliably in times of national crisis. PHIN encompasses four key components: (1) detection and monitoring; (2) analysis and interpretation; (3) information dissemination and knowledge management; and (4) public health response. Each of these components is briefly described below.

Public health information systems must support functions that include:

- Early event detection—BioSense (described later in this testimony) is being developed to support early event detection activities associated with a possible bioterrorism threat. Regional health data will be sent to authorized health officials detailing health trends that could be related to a possible bioterrorism attack.

- Routine public health surveillance—The National Electronic Disease Surveillance System (NEDSS) supports routine surveillance activities associated with the rapid reporting of disease trends to control outbreaks. The NEDSS platform allows states to enter, update and electronically transmit demographic and notifiable disease data.

- Secure communications among public health partners—The Epidemic Information Exchange, or Epi-X, technology allows for the secure exchange of communications among participating public health partners via the web by providing up-to-the-minute information, reports, alerts, and discussions about terrorist events, toxic exposures, disease outbreaks, and other public health events.

- Management and dissemination of information and knowledge—The Health Alert Network's architecture upgraded the capacity of state and local health agencies to communicate different health threats such as emerging infectious and chronic diseases, environmental hazards, as well as bioterrorism related threats.

- Other functions include—Analysis and interpretation of relevant public health data and public health response systems.

PHIN will provide the framework for these functions to serve as part of an integrated and interoperable network critical in establishing a more effective public health system.

Since the majority of the data management needs come after disease is detected, CDC through PHIN is investing in information systems to support our public health response teams and our Director's Emergency Operations Center (DEOC) in Atlanta and to assist state and local health agencies in tracking and managing vital public health information before, during, and after an event has occurred. CDC's DEOC,

## Robust Preparedness

Expanding the public health infrastructure toward incident preparedness has been a priority at the federal, state, and local levels over recent years. Most agencies build capacity and develop response plans in preparation against terrorist attacks and natural disasters . . .

When planning a preventive strategy, public health officials must be mindful of several factors paramount to mission success. As stated in the National Response Plan: Incident management cannot be event driven. The new paradigm must be approached through increased awareness, preventive measures, and robust preparedness. Preventing an incident from ever occurring reaps far more dividends than simply reducing the costs of post-incident response and recovery. In addition to avoidance of reactionary development of response plans, the efforts of public health agencies toward readiness and preparation have an innate difficulty. If there are no events during a time of preparedness expansion and readiness, it does not mean that we have successfully prepared for such occurrences, nor does it mean that we have wasted funding and public health resources in an effort that produced no measurable benefit.

Steven Alles, *"Perspective on Bioterrorism: Preparedness,*
*Risk Communication, and Psychological Health,"* Medscape, *2005.*

which opened in 2003, serves as the centralized facility for collaboration to gather and disseminate information to ensure a timely, coordinated and effective public health response.

## Biosurveillance Initiative

Recognizing the need to increase our current disease surveillance and detection capabilities, the President, on February 3, 2004, issued Homeland Security Presidential Directive 9 (HSPD-9), which states in part:

"The Secretary of Homeland Security shall coordinate with the Secretaries of Agriculture, Health and Human Services, and the Administrator of the Environmental Protection Agency, and the heads of other appropriate Federal departments and agencies to create a new biological threat awareness capacity that will enhance detection and characterization of an attack."

CDC's role in this biosurveillance initiative focuses on human health and involves three distinct but interrelated elements. The first is BioSense, a state-of-the-art, multijurisdictional data sharing program to facilitate surveillance of unusual patterns or clusters of disease around the country. This data sharing effort will support early detection of potential terrorism events while minimizing the reporting burden for state and local health departments and clinical personnel.

The second element of the initiative centers on the addition and expansion of quarantine stations at U.S. ports of entry and assigning multidisciplinary teams of quarantine officers, public health advisors, epidemiologists, and information technicians to these sites. This effort will assure effective monitoring of U.S. and international regulatory requirements for travelers, rapid communication of disease intelligence information to federal, state, local and international partners, and consistent supervision of clinical and research material movement through ports of entry.

The Laboratory Response Network, which serves as a point of integration for federal, state, local and territorial laboratories to ensure rapid and proficient laboratory diagnosis of emerging bioagents and environmental contaminants, is the third and final component of the biosurveillance initiative. Additional resources in FY 2005 will allow the Laboratory Response Network to expand its reach into food safety and animal diagnostic labs, thereby strengthening the nation's laboratory infrastructure for timely and accurate reporting of a potential bioterrorism attack.

The biosurveillance initiative is part of an interagency effort that crosses multiple sectors, including food supply, environmental monitoring, and human health surveillance, and its benefits will be felt in all state and local health departments. By integrating these otherwise isolated data sources, potential public health emergencies that may have gone undetected can be identified more rapidly. Through the biosurveillance initiative and ongoing capacity-building efforts at the state and local levels, the FY 2005 budget request will continue to enhance frontline emergency preparedness.

## Protecting the Nation's Health

CDC is committed to working with federal, state and local partners to protect the nation's health. Our best public health strategy against disease is the development, organization, and enhancement of public health disease detection systems, tools, and the people needed to wield them. The astute clinician remains the critical link in disease detection and reporting. The first case of West Nile in 1999, and the first case of anthrax reported in early October 2001, were identified by astute clinicians. Training and education of these front-line health protectors remain a high priority for CDC and will continue to be a priority as we strive to improve all components of the nation's disease detection systems.

While we have made substantial progress towards enhancing the nation's capability to rapidly detect disease within our communities, improving our response and containment strategies, and developing plans to recover from tragic events, much remains to be done. CDC is very grateful for the congressional support received to date and looks forward to continuing to work with Congress and Members of this committee as we strive to protect the public's health from terrorism and other public health emergencies.

*"Bioterrorism preparedness programs*
*have been a disaster for public health."*

# Bioterrorism Preparedness Programs Do Not Protect Public Health

*Hillel W. Cohen, Robert M. Gould, and Victor W. Sidel*

*In the following viewpoint, Hillel Cohen, Robert Gould, and Victor Sidel contend that bioterrorism preparedness programs have harmed public health and wasted billions of public health dollars. The authors point out that vaccination programs for anthrax and smallpox have contributed to illness and death, and secret biodefense laboratories pose more of a threat to the nation's public health than bioterrorism itself. Hillel Cohen and Victor Sidel are professors at Albert Einstein College of Medicine. Robert Gould is a doctor and the president of the organization Physicians for Social Responsibility.*

As you read, consider the following questions:

1. According to the authors, how many people who had cutaneous anthrax infections died?

Hillel W. Cohen, Robert M. Gould, and Victor W. Sidel, "The Pitfalls of Bioterrorism Preparedness: The Anthrax and Smallpox Experiences," *American Journal of Public Health*, vol. 94, October, 2004, pp. 1667–71. Reproduced by permission.

2. According to the authors, how many people suffered serious adverse events after taking the smallpox vaccine in phase 1? How many people died?

3. According to the authors, reports of accidents and mishandling of biological agents have occurred at what two biodefense facilities?

Recent bioterrorism preparedness programs that illustrate irrational and dysfunctional responses to inadequately characterized risks should be of urgent concern to all members of the public health community. Since anthrax spores were released in the US mail system in 2001 and caused 5 fatalities and widespread panic, the spores have been linked to a US military research programs suggesting that the release might not have occurred had the anthrax program never existed. The smallpox vaccination program has also been linked to fatalities and other serious adverse events, although evidence of risk of exposure to smallpox has been minimal. Indeed, the smallpox vaccination campaign may have been motivated by a political rather than health agenda. Continuing bioterrorism preparedness programs are similarly characterized by failure to apply reasonable priorities in the context of public health and failure to fully weigh the risks against the purported benefits of these programs. Such programs may cause substantial harm to the public health if allowed to proceed.

## Bioterrorism Preparedness Adversely Impacts Public Health

Efforts by the United States to prepare for the use of biological agents in war based on flawed evaluation of risks have had serious health consequences for military personnel and have led to significant weakening of international agreements against the use of biological agents. Massive campaigns focusing on "bioterrorism preparedness" have had adverse health consequences and have resulted in the diversion of essential public health personnel, facilities, and other resources from urgent, real public health needs. Preparedness proponents argued that allocating major resources to what were admittedly low-probability events would not represent wastefulness and would instead heighten public awareness and promote "dual use" funding that would serve other public health needs. Public health resources are woefully inadequate, and the notion that bioterrorism funding would bolster public health capability seemed plausible to many, even though we and others have argued that the "dual use" rationale is illusory. An evaluation of recent experience concerning anthrax and smallpox can help illuminate these issues.

## Improbable Anthrax Threat

Despite extensive work on the possible weaponization of anthrax, there has been no example of effective use of anthrax as a weapon of indiscriminant mass destruction. In 2001, shortly after the events of September 11, weapons-grade anthrax spores were mailed to several addressees, but none of the intended targets were injured. Of 11 people who developed inhalation anthrax, 5 died. Of the 12 who had cutaneous infections, all recovered after administration of antibiotics. Thousands of people in potentially exposed areas such as postal sorting centers were advised to use antibiotics prophytactically. Millions of people were terrified, and many thousands in areas where there was no possible risk of exposure also took antibiotics. Congress was closed for days, mail service was disrupted for months, and state and county public health laboratories were inundated with white powder samples that ranged from explicit anthrax hoaxes to spilled powdered sweeteners.

Despite early speculation linking the anthrax release to "foreign terrorists," evidence led investigators to suspect an individual who had been working in a US military facility that may have been in violation of the Biologic and Toxin Weapons Convention. Whether or not that specific individual was involved, it appears likely that the perpetrator or perpetrators were associated in some way with a US military program, that the motive for the extremely limited release was political, and that, without the existence of a US military laboratory, the material for the release would not have been available.

This experience supports the view that, as a consequence of the inherent difficulties in obtaining and handling such material, mass purposeful infection is highly improbable and the likely impact on morbidity and mortality limited. However, the nature of US "biodefense" programs may modify this prognosis; such programs may result in dangerous materials being more readily available, thus undermining the Biologic and Toxin Weapons Convention. Despite an absence of evidence of anthrax weapon stocks posing a threat to US military personnel, and despite problematic experiences of the military anthrax vaccination program, the US government announced plans to spend as much as $1.4 billion for millions of doses of an experimental anthrax vaccine that has not been proven safe or effective and the need for which has not been opened to public debate.

## Smallpox Vaccinations Political

The 2002–2003 campaign to promote smallpox as an imminent danger coincided with the Bush administration's preparations for war on Iraq and the now discredited claims that Iraq had amassed weapons of mass destruction and could launch a biological or chemical attack in "as little as 45 minutes." A media campaign describing the dangers of smallpox coincided with the buildup for the war. An unprecedented campaign advocating "pre-event" mass smallpox vaccinations, to be carried out in 2 phases—involving half a million members of the armed forces and half a million health workers in phase 1 and as many as 10 million emergency responders in phase 2—was announced in December 2002.

Before then, the debate on smallpox had been whether the stocks of stored stand-by vaccine were adequate or whether they should be increased. The World Health Organization (WHO), the Centers for Disease Control and Prevention (CDC), and virtually every public health official took the position that the vaccine involved too many adverse events—was too dangerous—to warrant mass vaccination when no case of smallpox existed or had existed for more than 20 years. When the Bush administration announced support for mass vaccinations, WHO did not change its position, but the CDC and other US public health officials and organizations, including the American Public Health Association (APHA), decided to acquiesce.

## Public Relations, Not Public Health Reasons

The coincidence of the Bush war calendar and the smallpox vaccination calendar, while not conclusive, is nonetheless consistent with an inference that the war agenda was the driving force behind the smallpox vaccination campaign. Since the invasion, evidence has emerged that allegations regarding Iraqi weapons of mass destruction were deliberate exaggerations or lies. The evidence is highly suggestive that the smallpox vaccination program was launched primarily for public relations rather than public health reasons.

## Deaths Inexcusable

The vaccination campaign did not proceed as planned. Opposition arose on both safety and political grounds, and most front-line health professionals simply did not volunteer to participate. Of the 500,000 health professionals who were targeted for inoculations in phase 1, fewer than 8% participated. Despite efforts to avoid vaccination of those who might be at elevated risk, the CDC reported that there were 145 serious

## Military Vaccination Is Morally Irresponsible

The War on Terror has become a droning drum beat that many believe exists solely for the purpose to benefit the pharmaceutical companies and their shareholders. If protection of the soldiers or the American people were actually the focus, then better detection and outer protective equipment would be the primary goal. It stands to reason that if an enemy knows a vaccine exists for a specific strain of biological warfare, a genetic alteration of that strain would render that vaccine useless. Where is the logic of spending billions of dollars on biopreparedness through vaccinations, where the only thing that is at least known is that it can become easily obsolete? . . .

The men and women who serve in our military may not be your sons or daughters, but they are someone's. As you think about the "Next Steps in Biopreparedness," please keep that in mind. Until then, my colleagues and I will continue to assist the soldiers and their families the best we can—those whose lives have already been destroyed, by just two of these biological vaccines.

The Government continues to try and find ways to combat terrorism and biological warfare. Aggressive measures should be taken; however, we need an honest and open assessment from all parties concerned regarding biopreparedness and the next steps, which goes beyond pharmaceutical companies and the NIH. Our nation is billions of dollars in debt, and spending billions of more dollars on biological vaccination programs that may fail on all counts, is financially and morally irresponsible.

*Randi Airola, Testimony to the U.S. Subcommittee on Bioterrorism and Public Health Preparedness, February 8, 2005. Available at: www.milvacs.org/P??CDOCS/randitest.doc.*

adverse events (resulting in hospitalization, permanent disability, life-threatening illness, or death) associated with smallpox vaccinations among civilians. Of these cases, at least 3 were deaths.

Three deaths resulting from thousands of inoculations would have been justifiable in preparation for a real threat of smallpox or in the midst of a smallpox outbreak, when vaccination could have saved many more lives. However, in the absence of any smallpox cases worldwide or any scientific basis for expecting an outbreak, these deaths and other serious adverse events are inexcusable. In August 2003, an Institute of Medicine committee that had been charged with reviewing the vaccination program came back to the position that had been generally accepted before 2002: that mass, prevent inoculations were unwarranted. According to the committee report:

> In the absence of any current benefit to individual vaccinees and the remote prospect of benefit in the future (as such benefit would be realized only in the event of a smallpox outbreak, and the outbreak occurred in the vaccinee's region), the balance of benefit to the individual and risk to others (through contact with the vaccinee or through disruption of other public health initiatives) becomes unfavorable. . . . In the absence of other forms of benefit, therefore, offering vaccination to members of the general public is contrary to the basic precepts of public health ethics.

The report further cited "lingering confusion about the vaccination program's aims." We find it difficult to comprehend how a program with confused aims and known serious risks can be viewed as having a positive risk-benefit ratio or how public health organizations could accept such a program without subjecting it to extensive critical examination and debate.

## Public Health Resources Drained

The smallpox vaccinations harmed others beyond those who suffered side effects. Considerable public health resources were used in the campaign. In a climate of state and local budget crises coinciding with the war and occupation, a downturn in employment, and a tax cut for the wealthy, public health services have been cut or are at serious risk. Funding for bioterrorism programs is not correcting the deficit, because such funds have been for the most part specifically earmarked for preparedness efforts and cannot be transferred to other public health programs. In general, federal increases in public health funding are much less extensive than state or local cuts. During the height of the smallpox vaccination effort, a number of state health officials complained that important work, including tuberculosis screening and standard children's inoculations, had to be scaled back. The siren song of dual use—that bioterrorism funding would strengthen public health infrastructure—has shown itself to be an empty promise, as preparedness priorities have weakened rather than strengthened public health.

## Secret Biodefense Labs Are Even Worse

Even worse, bioterrorism "preparedness" programs now under way include the development of a number of new secret research facilities that will store and handle dangerous materials, thus increasing the risk of accidental release or purposeful diversion. Reports of accidental leaks and improper disposal of hazardous wastes at the US Army facility at Fort Detrick serve as further warnings, as do revelations of mishandling of biological agents at the Plum Island, New York, facility that studies potential bioweapons that affect animals.

Most important, the proposed development of "biodefense" programs at sites, such as national nuclear weapons laboratories, that are traditionally secretive in their operations also provides an impetus for a potential global "biodefense race" that would likely spur proliferation of offensive biowarfare capabilities. Accidents or purposeful diversions from these facilities seem at least as likely as terrorist events, and perhaps more so, since the deadly materials are already present. The Patriot Act has greatly expanded the cloak of secrecy that shields these facilities from public awareness and oversight.

In short, bioterrorism preparedness programs have been a disaster for public health. Instead of leading to more resources for dealing with natural disease as had been promised, there are now fewer such resources. Worse, in response to bioterrorism preparedness, public health institutions and procedures are being reorganized along a military or police model that subverts the relationships between public health providers and the communities they serve.

## What Can Be Done?

What can we do? Advocacy groups and local coalitions have emerged to oppose the widespread siting of potentially dangerous bioterrorism laboratories and have demanded that such facilities be open to the public. Labor unions that helped resist the smallpox vaccinations can be vigilant against further efforts to enlist health workers in poorly conceived and misguided campaigns that pose unnecessary risks to patients, workers, and communities.

Above all, it is imperative that public health organizations such as APHA take a fresh and critical look at the government's biopreparedness agenda and advocate for a comprehensive program that promotes global health security. Such a program would initiate appropriate and focused preparedness efforts *only* in the context of concerted and cooperative international steps designed to reduce the likelihood of infection from all sources. The modalities employed would range from strengthened treaties to provision of adequate clean water, food, shelter, education, and health care for all. Those of us working in public health can insist on a reevaluation of the entire bioterrorism preparedness agenda and demand a close examination of its goals and consequences before additional resources are invested in programs that so far seem to have done more harm than good.

## Bioterrorism Preparedness Programs Have Done Harm

In light of the *daily toll* of thousands of deaths from illnesses and accidents that could be prevented with even modest increases in public health resources here and around the world, we believe that the huge spending on bioterrorism preparedness programs constitutes a reversal of any reasonable sense of priorities. While some still believe that bioterrorism preparedness programs will protect us from catastrophe, we agree with David M. Ozonoff, chairman emeritus of the Department of Environmental Health at the Boston University School of Public Health, that these programs represent "a catastrophe for American public health," and we hope it is not too late to change this dangerous direction.

War, poverty, environmental degradation, and misallocation of resources are the greatest root causes of worldwide mortality and morbidity, as well as ultimately being the underlying causes of terrorism itself. Bringing an awareness of this reality to the public is no easy task. However, one important step will be for the public health community to acknowledge the substantial harm that bioterrorism preparedness has already done and develop mechanisms both to increase our public health resources and to allocate them in a manner that will do the most good for all inhabitants of our increasingly fragile planet.

"The government's plan ... is based on the assumption that the population will wait quietly while the experts manage the epidemic ... It is more likely that people will demand vaccinations, perhaps storming health care institutions where vaccinations are being given."

# Mass Vaccination Would Be Necessary to Protect Against Smallpox Attack

*Edward P. Richards, Katharine C. Rathbun, and Jay Gold*

*In the following viewpoint, Edward Richards, Katharine Rathbun, and Jay Gold contend that in order to halt the spread of the smallpox virus, maintain civil order, and quell panic, the U.S. government should plan mass vaccinations. The authors say the U.S. government's 2003–2004 smallpox vaccination program, which was based on limited vaccinations, was a failure on many levels. They propose an alternative plan, which is based on quickly vaccinating as many people in the general public as possible. Edward P. Richards is a professor of law at Louisiana State University. Katharine Rathbun and Jay Gold are physicians.*

Edward P. Richards, Katharine C. Rathbun, Jay Gold, "The Smallpox Vaccination Campaign of 2003: Why Did It Fail and What Are the Lessons for Bioterrorism Preparedness?" *Louisiana Law Review*, Summer, 2004. Reproduced by permission. Available at http://biotech.law.lsu.edu/Articles/smallpox.pdf.

As you read, consider the following questions:

1. According to the authors, what was the biggest unknown about the U.S. government's 2003–2004 smallpox vaccination plan?
2. According to the authors, what was demonstrated in the 1947 New York smallpox campaign?
3. According to the authors, what are the two benefits of rapidly vaccinating as many people as possible?

On December 13, 2002, the White House announced a plan to vaccinate active duty military personnel and certain civilian hospital, health care, and emergency services workers against smallpox. . . . The goal was to vaccinate 500,000 military personnel as soon as possible, and then to vaccinate 500,000 civilians within a few weeks. There were no specific plans to vaccinate the general population, but there was discussion about making the smallpox vaccine available to the general public in 2004. President Bush was immunized first, with no reported ill effects.

By January 2004, 578,286 military personnel were vaccinated. During the same period, only 39,213 civilian health-care and public health workers were vaccinated, less than ten percent of the original goal. This article analyzes why the civilian smallpox vaccination campaign failed, the impact of this failure, and what it should teach us about future vaccination campaigns for smallpox and other bioterrorism agents. . . .

## Was Vaccination Worth the Risk?

The biggest unknown about the smallpox vaccination plan was the risk of an outbreak of smallpox versus the risk of the vaccination plan. Unfortunately, of course, probability information is impossible to obtain for bioterrorist activities. As discussed previously, smallpox is more problematic than most possible bioterror agents because there is no clear evidence that the virus is available to terrorists. Unlike agents such as anthrax and plague, which are readily available because they are used by many laboratories and because they have animal reservoirs, smallpox virus will be available only if it has been diverted from the Soviet bioweapons program. It is assumed that this information was kept from the CDC and other public health experts until the late 1990s because the government did not think it posed a significant threat. Had there been a decision in 1993 that smallpox posed a threat, work should have begun then on a safe alternative vaccine.

The announcement of the smallpox vaccination plan was not accompanied by any information about why smallpox now had become a priority, and in fact, the announcement stated that there was no new, specific risk. There were heated debates in 1972 about whether smallpox vaccinations should be stopped, with a significant faction arguing that ending vaccinations would eventually create an environment that would support a global pandemic of smallpox.

That fear has now come to pass, with the events of 9/11 reopening the debate about the wisdom of continuing a world that is susceptible to smallpox. If there is a real risk of smallpox, then perhaps the question should be whether we resume routine vaccinations for healthy persons, not whether we will vaccinate a small group of volunteers. If a safer vaccine is developed, resuming smallpox vaccinations might make sense. With the current vaccine, on the other hand, the politics of immunosuppression secondary to HIV complicates the risk calculus—will it really be possible to protect immunosuppressed persons from vaccination and secondary spread while keeping their immune status secret?

## Should Have Recruited Vaccinating Volunteers

The best rationale for the smallpox vaccination plan was to prepare a cadre of medical care providers and front-line emergency services providers who could deal with cases of smallpox as part of community response teams. If a smallpox case was identified, teams could focus on the patients while other health care workers were being vaccinated and were vaccinating others. This could have been accomplished if the plan had been set up to recruit volunteers with specific skills. Such volunteers would have been vaccinated by the health department personnel, would have been kept away from direct patient care until the vaccine sore had healed, and would have been assured of adequate compensation if they were injured. This would have solved the worker's compensation and liability issues for the hospitals, and would have addressed the volunteers' fears about whether they would be compensated if injured. By focusing on a team for the community, rather than requiring each hospital to have its own team, relatively few health care workers would have been needed, which would have reduced the cost of carrying out the plan.

## Should Have Designated Vaccination Facilities

Instead, the plan was oriented to individual hospitals, on the assumption that smallpox patients would be flooding the hospital emergency rooms and would be treated at every hospital. There were no distinctions drawn between general acute care hospitals and specialty hospitals such as cancer treatment centers which do not take walk-in patients. Vaccinated health care workers would care for these patients in their hospitals. This plan makes no provision for the other patients in the hospital. Hospitals have a very limited number of isolation beds suitable for smallpox, and almost no hospitals have a safe way to transport patients from the front door into those rooms without exposing others. If there are more than a small number of smallpox cases, a hospital will no longer be able to isolate them. At that point all the other patients and unvaccinated staff would have to be moved out and the facility converted to a smallpox hospital, or the smallpox patients would have to be sent away.

Smallpox cases should not be admitted or treated in every hospital in the community. They should be sent to designated regional smallpox hospitals. To minimize the risk of secondary spread of smallpox, a regional smallpox hospital should not house a significant number of immunosuppressed persons. There should be a plan for how to evacuate all patients and unimmunized staff to other facilities should smallpox be identified in the community. Ideally, a regional hospital should be run by a government entity that is shielded from lawsuits by sovereign immunity. This would allow compensation under a tort claims act. These regional hospitals should be federal hospitals such as Veterans Administration hospitals because the government has the best tort law protection and the best ability to absorb other costs such as worker's compensation claims. More importantly, a federal facility will be able to absorb the tremendous financial risks of treating smallpox cases, including the potential closing of the facility if decontamination proves impossible. This is important even if the Homeland Security Act immunity is in place to prevent tort claims.

The plan also fails to deal with the health care workers who cannot be immunized. These workers will have to be kept away from any possible smallpox cases for their own safety and because unimmunized health care workers are a prime way to spread smallpox. If the country is in a constant state of readiness for a smallpox outbreak, does this mean that such workers cannot be in any jobs where they might encounter an undiagnosed smallpox case? If there is a case identified in the community, should all unimmunized workers be sent home? Who will cover their duties? What about health care workers outside of hospitals? Patients are as likely to go to private physicians as to hospital-based clinics. How should such facilities handle potential smallpox cases? . . .

## Providing for Mass Vaccinations Is a Better Plan

Unlike most vaccines, the smallpox vaccine is fully effective up to three days after a person is exposed to the virus, and somewhat effective for a few days more. This is because the incubation time for smallpox is much longer than for the vaccinia in the vaccine. The vaccine sore develops quickly, driving the production of antibodies that then prevent the smallpox virus from gaining a foothold in the patient. This provides a window of opportunity to vaccinate persons after exposure and still stop the development of smallpox in most of them. Given the uncertain, but low, probability of a smallpox outbreak in any given city, and at any given hospital, an alternative to prophylactic vaccination is to wait until there is a case of smallpox and then be prepared to vaccinate people very quickly.

## Many People Can Be Quickly Vaccinated

As was demonstrated in the 1947 New York smallpox vaccination campaign and others around the world, large numbers of people can be vaccinated in a short period of time. Dealing with health care providers is the simplest case. Vaccine could be stockpiled locally, even at the hospital and clinic level. It is stable and easy to store, but would need to be secured. The technique for performing the vaccination is very simple, having been designed to be done by unskilled workers after very limited training. The current recommendations are focused on a zero risk approach, i.e., elaborate recordkeeping, detailed informed consent, and extensive safety precautions to prevent the person performing the vaccination from being exposed to vaccinia. These are appropriate precautions for prophylactic vaccinations when there have been no reported cases of smallpox.

The risk calculus shifts dramatically as soon as there are active cases of smallpox in the community. At that point, the risk of not being vaccinated and developing smallpox is much greater than the risk of vaccine complications for all but the most severely immunocompromised individuals. The risk of exposure to vaccinia becomes much less significant when most people will already be exposed to vaccinia through vaccinations. Even in hospitals, most patients would be candidates for vaccination in an outbreak, and for those who are not, the low risk of vaccinia exposure from vaccinated health care

## Smallpox Disease

Smallpox is a serious, contagious, and sometimes fatal infectious disease. There is no specific treatment for smallpox disease, and the only prevention is vaccination. The name *smallpox* is derived from the Latin word for "spotted" and refers to the raised bumps that appear on the face and body of an infected person.

There are two clinical forms of smallpox. Variola major is the severe and most common form of smallpox, with a more extensive rash and higher fever. There are four types of variola major smallpox: ordinary (the most frequent type, accounting for 90% or more of cases); modified (mild and occurring in previously vaccinated persons); flat; and hemorrhagic (both rare and very severe). Historically, variola major has an overall fatality rate of about 30%; however, flat and hemorrhagic smallpox usually are fatal. Variola minor is a less common presentation of smallpox, and a much less severe disease, with death rates historically of 1% or less.

Smallpox outbreaks have occurred from time to time for thousands of years, but the disease is now eradicated after a successful worldwide vaccination program. The last case of smallpox in the United States was in 1949. The last naturally occurring case in the world was in Somalia in 1977. After the disease was eliminated from the world, routine vaccination against smallpox among the general public was stopped because it was no longer necessary for prevention.

*U.S. Centers for Disease Control and Prevention (CDC)*
*Smallpox Fact Sheet; Smallpox Overview, August 9, 2004.*
*Available at www.cdc.gov/smallpox.*

workers would be much less than the risk of spread of the disease by unvaccinated workers. Stripped of the paperwork requirements, and with an adequate supply of vaccine and the bifurcated needles used to administer it, smallpox vaccinations take little time. A handful of nurses could train others very quickly, then fan out and vaccinate every health care worker in a facility. The same could be done by EMTs in ambulance services and in clinics. With the supplies in place ahead of time, some basic training, and a shift from worrying about vaccine injuries to worrying about smallpox, it should be possible to vaccinate health care workers very quickly.

## Public Will Demand Vaccine

The most important question in smallpox vaccination policy is how to handle the public demand for vaccinations. Under the federal government's current ring immunization plan, cases will be investigated, as will all the contacts to the cases, and contacts will be vaccinated and isolated for two weeks to make sure that they do not develop smallpox. It is likely that the media will announce the smallpox cases to the world before local emergency preparedness personnel are all notified. The first question they will likely ask will be, "where and how does everyone get vaccinated?"

Under a ring immunization plan, the answer is that the general public should not worry about getting vaccinated. Only persons in contact with a smallpox case or working in health care or emergency services should be vaccinated. Unfortunately, the vaccination of health care workers cannot be carried out in isolation from the rest of the population. Even with a cadre of pre-vaccinated health care workers, the rest of the health care work force would need to be vaccinated as soon as smallpox cases are identified in the community. Once the vaccination of health care workers starts, they will want their families, and then their friends, vaccinated. Once it hits the news that there are cases of smallpox and that people are being vaccinated, it is the authors' prediction that most of the population will want to be vaccinated. The federal government's plan, on the other hand, is based on the assumption that the population will wait quietly while the experts manage the epidemic.

Waiting quietly during an epidemic of one of history's great killers does not seem likely. It is more likely that people will demand vaccinations, perhaps storming health care institutions where vaccinations are being given. People will also want to flee, which is a rational response to smallpox. Not being able to obtain vaccinations may exacerbate the pressure to flee, further complicating efforts to keep the disease from being carried to new locations. It is likely that politicians will demand that the general public have access to smallpox vaccinations—the only question is how much public panic will there be before the order is given. Once vaccinations are available, it is critical that everyone who wants one be able to obtain it very quickly. A requirement that people wait for several days at a vaccination clinic, as contemplated in the federal mass vaccination plan, seems an invitation to public disorder.

Rather than a plan based on a relatively small number of vaccination clinics, with paperwork and consent requirements, everyone who can be trained to give smallpox vaccinations should be sent into the community to give them. The vaccinations should be given where people are, such as schools, churches, shopping centers, and sports stadiums. If the area is blanketed with people with vaccine, creating a public perception that everyone who wants it can obtain it, the public order problem will be lessened considerably. While many people will still want to flee, this approach may reduce the pressure to leave.

## Benefits of Mass Vaccination

There are two benefits of rapidly vaccinating as many people as possible. First, it would be more likely that there will be enough herd immunity [i.e. group immunity] to stop the outbreak, even though not all second generation cases will have been eliminated. While there may still be many deaths, public order is more likely to be preserved. Second, and much more controversially, it means that more people would be vaccinated before reports of real and alleged vaccine-related injuries are publicized. This is critical if the federal government is to keep its promise that no one will be vaccinated against her/his will. If too many people decline vaccination, the choice may be between forced vaccinations and failure to stop the epidemic.

*"The rate of severe illness and death caused by the vaccine itself would cancel out any benefit from mass vaccination."*

# Mass Vaccination Is Unnecessary to Protect Against Smallpox

## Ira Longini and Elizabeth Halloran

*In the following viewpoint, a smallpox vaccination study performed by Ira Longini and Elizabeth Halloran of the Fred Hutchinson Cancer Research Center is described. Using a computer modeling program that calculated the spread of Variola virus disseminated in a "virtual" U.S. city, the scientists found that mass vaccination is unnecessary in the event of a smallpox outbreak. The authors say that immediate quarantine of infected individuals along with limited vaccination of their close contacts and frontline health care workers is sufficient to thwart a smallpox epidemic. Ira Longini and Elizabeth Halloran are faculty members at the Fred Hutchinson Cancer Research Center, a nonprofit biomedical research institute in Seattle, WA.*

"Study Finds Mass Vaccination Unnecessary in the Event of a Large-Scale Bioterrorist Smallpox Attack in the United States," *Fred Hutchinson Cancer Research Center*, October 16, 2006. Reproduced by permission. Available at www.fhcrc.org/about/ne/news/2006/10/16/smallpox.html.

As you read, consider the following questions:

1. What is the name of the committee that was convened by the Secretary's Advisory Council on Public Health Preparedness?

2. According to the authors, one in every how many persons will have a severe reaction to the smallpox vaccine? One in how many persons will die?

3. How many people lived in Longini's and Halloran's virtual community?

Mass vaccination would not be necessary in the event of a large-scale small bioterrorist attack in the United States, according to a study led by researchers at Fred Hutchinson Cancer Research Center that appears online in the *International Journal of Infectious Diseases*.

Instead, the current U.S. government policy of post-release surveillance, prompt containment of victims and vaccination of hospital workers and close contacts would be sufficient to thwart an epidemic, according to lead author Ira M. Longini Jr., Ph.D., a world leader in using mathematical and statistical methods to study the natural course of infectious diseases.

"We found that a well-prepared response of surveillance and containment, if done quickly, within a day or two of detecting the first smallpox case, would contain a large attack if up to 500 people were infected," said Longini, a member of the Public Health Sciences Division at the Hutchinson Center and a professor of biostatistics at the University of Washington School of Public Health and Community Medicine. These results apply to scenarios involving even the most virulent, fatal forms of the virus.

However, Longini emphasizes, failure to quickly isolate known smallpox cases and vaccinate their close contacts could thwart the containment of an epidemic.

## Vaccination of Close Contacts Sufficient

These findings emerge from a committee of smallpox experts—including infectious-disease modelers, epidemiologists, statisticians and clinicians—who were commissioned by former Secretary of Health and Human Services Tommy Thompson to evaluate a variety of intervention strategies to determine whether the United States could contain a large-scale smallpox bioterrorist attack and, if so, how.

Specifically, the researchers were charged with determining whether surveillance and containment—isolation of detected smallpox cases and vaccination of their close contacts—would be sufficient to contain a large attack. They also wanted to find out whether other interventions, such as mass pre-vaccination of the general public, pre-vaccination of hospital personnel, vaccination of the target community and closure of schools after a smallpox release would help contain the spread of the disease.

Thompson's senior science adviser, Donald Ainslie (D.A.) Henderson, the physician and epidemiologist who oversaw the World Health Organization's successful campaign to eradicate smallpox from the world in the late 1970s, served as a consultant to the committee, known as the Smallpox Modeling Working Group. The group was convened by the Secretary's Advisory Council on Public Health Preparedness, a branch of the U.S. Department of Health and Human Services.

## Vaccine Risks Cancel Out Mass Vaccination Gains

"Earlier studies recommended mass pre-vaccination of the general population to protect against a smallpox attack. None of us on the committee believed this was necessary, including D.A. Henderson, who intimately understands the natural history of the virus," Longini said. "The secretary of Health and Human Services wanted to settle such issues regarding smallpox containment once and for all, and this was our charge."

While the researchers did find that mass vaccination would slightly reduce the number of deaths from smallpox, they also found that the rate of severe illness and death caused by the vaccine itself would cancel out any benefit from mass vaccination. One person in 10,000 will have a severe reaction and one in a million will die from the vaccine, Longini said.

"Precautionary vaccination of hospital personnel and post-release vaccination of the target population would further contain the spread of smallpox, but at a cost of many more people being vaccinated," said co-author and Hutchinson Center biostatistician M. Elizabeth (Betz) Halloran, M.D., D.Sc. "The financial cost and potential illness and death related to vaccination must be weighed against the potential benefits in the event of an attack. In our opinion, pre-vaccination of the population at large is unnecessary," she said.

Longini, Halloran and colleagues also found that closure of schools after a smallpox attack would have a minimal effect in preventing transmission of the disease, and that any delay in quarantining infected individuals would take a much greater toll on the community than failing to pre-vaccinate potential cases.

## Studied Virtual Community

To conduct the study, Longini and colleagues created a computer model that calculated the spread of smallpox via aerosol dissemination—the most likely choice of terrorists—within a community of 50,000. Members of this virtual community interacted the way people normally do: within households, neighborhoods, preschool groups, schools, a community hospital and the community at large. The age distribution and household sizes were based on the U.S. census for 2000.

Predicting the spread of an infectious disease such as smallpox requires much more than simply connecting dots on a map. Instead Longini and colleagues rely on a tool called stochastic modeling to take into account real-world unpredictability, as well as many factors about the disease and the affected population. In constructing these models, Longini and colleagues begin with assumptions about how people interact and how the virus spreads. They also introduce and evaluate the effectiveness of various intervention strategies.

The study represents the first attempt to integrate what science knows about the natural history of smallpox—how various forms of the disease manifest over time—with human patterns of behavior to construct the most-comprehensive model of a smallpox epidemic to date.

"If smallpox appeared in Seattle tomorrow, which it could do, I'm absolutely confident that we could contain it if our recommendations for surveillance and containment were put into practice. I rest easier now that we've done this study," Longini said. "The process was kind of like unveiling the enemy to the point where we really understood it. This research has helped us demystify the threat a bit."

## Smallpox Caused by Variola Virus

Although smallpox has been eliminated as a naturally-occurring disease, the virus still exists in two approved laboratories in the United States and Russia. The Centers for Disease Control and Prevention classifies it as a "Category A" agent, presenting the greatest potential threat for harming public health if developed and used as a bioterrorist agent.

Smallpox is caused by the variola virus, which emerged thousands of years ago. Variola major, the most common form of the virus, is divided into four subcategories: ordinary (which accounts for about 90 percent of cases and has a fatality rate of about 30 percent), modified (which occurs in people who have been vaccinated and has a death rate of about 10 percent), and flat and hemorrhagic (both very rare and uniformly fatal).

According to the CDC, exposure to the variola virus is followed by an incubation period of seven to 17 days, during

## Smallpox Eradication Used Ring Vaccination

During [Donald A.] Henderson's tenure as [World Health Organization] (WHO's) chief medical officer for its global [smallpox] eradication program, smallpox cases were generally limited to Brazil, South Asia and most parts of Africa. WHO workers identified outbreaks readily, because every victim had a visible rash and almost every survivor was left with pockmarks. "If we went into a brand-new area, we could quickly tell whether they had any smallpox there or not," says Henderson. "We could look on the faces of people and know." Most people who were asked "When did you get those scars?" knew the year precisely. A brush with smallpox, he says, "was a very memorable event."

In the late 1960s and early '70s, conventional wisdom held that the way to eradicate a disease was to vaccinate entire populations. But Henderson thought that for smallpox, such a strategy would be expensive, tedious—and unnecessary. Instead, he used an approach known as ring vaccination. When a case was identified, the sick person was isolated quickly, and vaccine was given to all of the patient's primary contacts (relatives, neighbors, co-workers) and secondary contacts (the contacts of the contacts). In this way, outbreaks could be throttled with a vaccination rate of 50 to 80 percent.

The strategy worked. In October 1977, a young man in Somalia named Ali Maow Maalin became the last human case of naturally occurring smallpox in the world. (He survived.) In 1980, WHO declared the disease eradicated.

*Robin Marantz Henig, "D.A. Henderson: Eradicating One of History's Deadliest Diseases Was Just the Beginning,"*
Smithsonian, *November, 2005.*

which people are not contagious and feel fine. The first symptoms emerge during what is called the prodrome phase, and they include head and body aches, fatigue, a high fever and, sometimes, vomiting. This phase lasts two to four days and at this point people may or may not be contagious. Then a rash emerges all over the body and grows increasingly severe over the next 20 or so days, eventually forming scabs; during this period people are contagious, particularly during the first seven to 10 days of the rash. The disease eventually resolves and contagion ends after all of the scabs have fallen off. People who survive are then considered to be immune from smallpox.

A person can become infected by prolonged, face-to-face exposure with someone who is contagious, direct contact with infected bodily fluids or a contaminated object, such as bedding or clothing, and exposure to an aerosol release.

Routine smallpox vaccination ended in 1972, which leaves at least 43 percent of the U.S. population unvaccinated, Longini said. Research suggests that those previously vaccinated may still have substantial residual immunity although, if infected, they could still transmit the virus to others. Those most vulnerable to the virus are the very young and those whose immune systems are compromised due to HIV/AIDS, cancer or some other medical condition. An estimated 50 million Americans fall into this category, Longini said.

"*Public health systems are already much stronger and better prepared for bioterrorism.*"

# The United States Is Prepared to Respond to Bioterrorism

### *The U.S. Department of Health and Human Services (HHS)*

*In the following viewpoint, the U.S. Department of Health and Human Services (HHS) says it has made several accomplishments in regard to bioterrorism preparedness, and the nation is better prepared today. Increased hospital preparedness, nationwide health-care training, and swift progress in biodefense research are among the many accomplishments HHS declares. The HHS claims that much of the nation's preparedness progress is due to "Biodefense for the 21st Century," a presidential directive issued by President Bush. HHS is the United States government's principal agency for "protecting the health of all Americans and providing essential human services."*

As you read, consider the following questions:

1. According to the Department of Health and Human Services (HHS), how many states have bioterrorism response plans in place?

The U.S. Department of Health and Human Services (HHS), "HHS Accomplishment in Biodefense Preparedness," February 21, 2006. Available at www.hhs.gov/news/factsheet/biodefense.html.

2. According to the HHS, how does "Biosense" advance the nation's capability for early event detection?

3. The National Institutes of Health (NIH) developed a fast-acting vaccine and is testing its efficacy in humans for what virus?

President Bush has made strengthening the nation's defenses against biological weapons a critical national priority. While significant progress has been made, the President instructed federal departments and agencies to review their efforts and find new and better ways to secure America from bioattacks. The result of this review was *"Biodefense for the 21st Century,"* a Presidential directive that provides a comprehensive framework for our nation's biodefense. . . . "Biodefense for the 21st Century" builds on past accomplishments, specifies roles and responsibilities, and integrates the programs and efforts of various communities—national security, medical, public health, intelligence, diplomatic, agricultural and law enforcement—into a sustained and focused national effort against biological weapons threats. "Biodefense for the 21st Century" outlines the essential pillars of our biodefense program and provides specific directives to further strengthen the significant gains put in place during the past three years. At HHS, in cooperation with the Department of Homeland Security, preparations have included the following highlights: . . .

## State and Local Public Health Agencies Are Stronger

An unprecedented partnership effort with states and hospitals was launched quickly.

- A total of $3.6 billion has been made available for state, local and hospital preparedness since 2001.

- Funds go through state public health agencies, but 75 percent will ultimately go for direct or indirect support of local public health departments and hospitals.

- States are drawing these funds as quickly as they are able to ramp up their preparedness efforts and invest the money productively.

Public health systems are already much stronger and better prepared for bioterrorism and other mass casualty incidents.

- All 50 states have bioterrorism response plans in place.

- Ninety-eight percent of states have individuals assigned to receive and evaluate urgent disease reports 24 hours a day, 7 days a week, 365 days a year (24/7/365) and all states have protocols in place to activate the public health emergency response system 24/7/365.

- All states have plans in place for receiving and distributing assets from the Strategic National Stockpile and are implementing those plans.

- Twenty-one pilot cities, plus 15 new cities, are receiving funding through CDC's Cities Readiness Initiative (CRI) to develop plans for dispensing mass prophylaxis to their entire population within 48 hours.

- States are updating their laws for dealing with public health emergencies, using the draft model legislation on emergency health powers that was prepared at CDC's request. As of June 2005, 37 states and the District of Columbia have passed bills or resolutions related to the draft model legislation.

More workers and expertise have been directed at public health emergency preparedness.

- CDC awards fund over 3,500 state and local public health staff working full or part time on emergency preparedness activities.

- HHS staff dedicated to public health emergency preparedness is now 1,700, up from 212 in FY 2001. [In 2007], the number will rise again, to over 2,000.

- CDC will complete training in emergency preparedness and response for approximately 400 existing staff assigned to state and local public health agencies by 2006.

- CDC continues to provide expert assistance, especially through its "disease detectives," the Epidemic Intelligence Service (EIS). This two-year program has 149 EIS officers available to respond to biodefense and other public health emergencies.

America's public health laboratory capacity, a crucial element in detecting and understanding any disease outbreak, is greatly expanding.

- The Laboratory Response Network, connecting labs of many kinds that can help in an emergency, has been expanded to 142 member labs in all 50 states and several international sites, up from 91 labs in 2001.

- CDC has trained more than 8,800 clinical laboratorians to play a role in the detection, diagnostics, and reporting of public health emergencies.

- Fifteen new high-level biocontainment research laboratories are being funded by the [National Institutes of Health] NIH primarily for extramural research purposes, but they would also be available to assist in public health response to bioterrorism or infectious disease emergencies.

Communications capacity within the public health structure has been expanded and improved.

- CDC's Public Health Information Network Partner Communication capacity can reach 1 million recipients quickly, including 86 percent of all state public health agencies.

- BioSense, a component of CDC's Public Health Information Network, advances the nation's capabilities for early event detection by providing real-time data from hospitals and other facilities, has been made available to 34 city jurisdictions and 50 states, and supports over 330 users in all states and major metropolitan areas.

- CDC's [Epidemic Information Exchange] EPI-X system also connects more than 3,600 public health officials nationwide for immediate sharing of emergent public health data, compared with 200 in 2001.

- These improvements will help make public communications clearer and faster in an emergency.

## Hospitals and Health-care Providers Are Better Prepared

Hospital preparedness efforts have resulted in new state- and region-wide coordination, with coherent plans for investment and response.

- A new nationwide program, developed after the Sept. 11, 2001, terrorist attacks, has initiated planning processes in all states and territories to bolster the capacity of hospitals to deliver coordinated and effective care to victims of terrorism and other public health emergencies.

- Through [Health Resources and Services Administration] HRSA's National Bioterrorism Hospital Preparedness Program, ... hospitals and supporting healthcare systems receive funds to augment the number of hospital beds that can be used in a large-scale public health emergency; increase and expand hospital and regional isolation capacity; enhance hospital-based pharmaceutical stocks, and plan for community-wide disease prevention efforts.

- Program funds also are used to identify additional health care personnel who would be called on in a mass casualty incident, which may include terrorism, accidents or naturally occurring disease, and to increase behavioral health training and triage for all health care personnel.

- All states have developed plans with their hospitals for dealing with mass casualty incidents, including terrorism, accidents or naturally-occurring diseases.

Nationwide training for health care professionals is being implemented, and scientific expertise is growing.

- Almost 174,000 health professionals [were] trained in FY 2003 and 2004 through HRSA's Bioterrorism Training and Curriculum Development program, with 19 grants for continuing education aimed at the diverse health care workforce, and 13 grants to health professions schools to develop curricula.

- NIH's new Regional Centers of Excellence (RCEs) for Biodefense and Emerging Infectious Diseases will build a strong intellectual infrastructure for research and development while also developing our base of scientific expertise by training a new generation of science professionals to perform Biodefense research.

- CDC's Centers for Public Health Preparedness (CPHPs) help prepare frontline health workers at the local level. There are now 41 CPHPs in 46 states, comprised of schools of public health, schools of medicine and other local institutions. The CPHP has delivered over 380 preparedness education activities, reaching over 250,000 learners nationwide.

Federal emergency resources have been expanded to back-up local resources when they become overwhelmed.

- The Strategic National Stockpile now includes twelve 50-ton "12-hour Push Packages," up from eight in 2001. The amount and variety of stockpile contents has also grown. It now contains increased amounts of antibiotic prophylactic regimens for anthrax and the inventory goal has risen from 12 million in 2003 to 50 million in 2005.

- The National Disaster Medical System has 33 percent more personnel for its emergency response teams—8,000 personnel today, up from 6,000 in 2001.

- HHS has quadrupled the Readiness Force in the U.S. Public Health Service Commissioned Corps, from 600 in 2001 to almost 2,300.

## Food Safety Enhancements

[The U.S. Food and Drug Administration] FDA is implementing the most fundamental enhancements of its food safety activities in many years.

- FDA has more than doubled its presence at ports of entry, from 40 ports in 2001 to 90 ports.

- In 2006, FDA is performing 60,000 inspections of imported foods, five times more than in 2001. In FY 2005, FDA proposes to conduct 97,000 inspections, eight times higher than 2001.

- FDA is implementing its new authority for registration of food facilities (*some 425,000 are expected to register*); for prior notification of food import shipment (*some 20,000 notices per day expected*); for record-keeping to identify the immediate previous sources and immediate subsequent recipients of food; and for administrative detention of suspected foods.

- FDA has created a Food Emergency Response Network, with 63 labs representing 34 states—no such network existed in 2001.

## CDC Focusing on "All-Hazards" Preparedness

Since 2001, CDC and the nation as a whole have made great progress in preparing for catastrophic events—whether the event is a bioterror attack, an influenza pandemic, a hurricane, or other man-made or natural event. We've learned that preparation for one type of event can provide lessons to prepare for another. By focusing on "all-hazards" preparedness, federal, state, and local partners are able to use their limited resources to prepare comprehensively for as many threats as possible. CDC and its partners have accomplished much, and there is much left to do.

*Julie Gerberding, Director CDC, Testimony to the U.S. Committee on Appropriations, U.S. House of Representatives, March 9, 2007.*

- FDA is expanding its eLEXNET communications network for immediate exchange of critical food testing data. [In 2001], there are 108 laboratories representing 49 states and the District of Columbia. They are capable of dealing with more than 3,700 analytes. In 2000, there were eight labs, capable of tracking a sole analyte.

## Biodefense Research

The Biodefense research initiative is the largest single increase in resources for any initiative in the history of NIH.

- Biodefense research funding at NIH has increased from $53 million in FY 2001 to $1.6 billion in FY 2004.

- The increased effort is guided by strategic plans and research agendas developed with the guidance of panels of scientific experts.

167

- More than 50 biodefense initiatives have been developed to address research and development priorities in therapeutics, vaccines, diagnostics, and basic research including genomics, proteomics and bioinformatics.

- NIH has invested more than $800 million for the construction of 15 extramural labs and three intramural labs, and physical security. These are critical to developing countermeasures against agents of bioterror.

- NIH will emphasize product development and cooperative enterprises with private industry and academia, in addition to its traditional role of supporting basic scientific research.

Progress in Biodefense research has been swift and substantial.

New and improved vaccines against smallpox, anthrax, and other potential bioterror agents are being developed and evaluated and will soon enter the national stockpile through Project BioShield.

- NIH rapidly developed a fast-acting Ebola virus vaccine and showed its efficacy in monkeys; it is now being tested in human volunteers.

- NIH-supported scientists have identified antivirals that may play a role in treating smallpox or the complications of smallpox vaccination, as well as new antibiotics and antitoxins against other major bioterror threats.

- NIH has established ten Regional Centers of Excellence for Biodefense and Emerging Infectious Diseases Research (RCE). This nationwide group of multidisciplinary centers is a key element in the HHS strategic plan for biodefense research.

- NIH has supported the genomic sequencing of all bacteria (including the anthrax bacterium) considered to be bioterror threats, as well as the sequencing of genomes for at least one strain of every potential viral and protozoan bioterror pathogen.

Capacity is being expanded to produce medical countermeasures to protect Americans from bioterrorism attacks.

- The supply of smallpox vaccine has increased from 15.4 million doses available in 2001, to more than 300 million full doses today, enough to vaccinate every American, if necessary.

- The President has launched the BioShield initiative, to create a more stable and assured source of funding to purchase new vaccines or treatments. BioShield will provide $5.6 billion over the next 10 years for new products. FDA has approved new medical countermeasures, including therapies for anthrax, radiation exposure and antidotes to nerve agent poisoning. FDA has also implemented programs to facilitate development of new products.

- In the past four years, FDA finalized the "animal rule," which provides for using animals to test the safety and efficacy of products where human tests would be unfeasible. This rule can be important in the development of many Biodefense countermeasures.

Federal coordination and capacity has been expanded.

- The Department of Homeland Security creates a focal point for federal leadership.

- HHS has created a top-level Office of Public Health Emergency Preparedness to coordinate Department-wide efforts.

- HHS operating divisions work closely with states, providing specific performance measures and benchmarks, with semi-annual review of progress. HHS' Office of

Inspector General is also increasing its activities to ensure proper accounting and expenditure of federal support.

- In collaboration with the Department of Justice, CDC launched the "Forensic Epidemiology" course to train frontline public health, public safety and law enforcement professionals to conduct effective joint investigations.

## Helping People Cope with Terrorism

Mental Health and Substance Abuse Preparedness has been enhanced at the State and Local level.

- [Substance Abuse and Mental Health Services Administration] SAMHSA developed cooperative agreements with 35 States to enhance State-level capacity for a coordinated response to large-scale emergencies. These 2-year planning grants for about $100,000 annually are helping States with substance abuse and mental health preparedness, planning, training, technical assistance, and coordination. States are currently finalizing their plans for submission to SAMHSA.

- In 2003, SAMHSA sponsored *Creating a Roadmap for Disaster Preparedness: Strengthening State Capacity for Disaster Mental Health and Substance Abuse*. Representatives of over 50 States and territories attended this meeting, which was followed by a series of six regional planning meetings for State and community-level agencies.

- In October 2002, SAMHSA hosted a multi-State meeting, *Forum for 9/11 State Disaster Relief Grantees*. State teams could include mental health, substance abuse, emergency response, and community representatives.

The meeting aimed to share State experiences and lessons learned, review programmatic findings and make recommendations.

- In June 2003, SAMHSA released the comprehensive *Mental Health All-Hazards Disaster Planning Guidance* for use by States and local communities. In 2004, SAMHSA collaborated with the Office for Victims of Crime in the U.S. Department of Justice to produce *Mental Health Response to Mass Violence and Terrorism: A Training Manual.*

*"Five years after 9/11, public health pre-*
*paredness falls far short of what is re-*
*quired to protect the American people."*

# The United States Is
# Not Prepared to Respond
# to Bioterrorism

*Jeffrey Levi, Laura M. Segal, Emily Gandola, Chrissie Juliano,*
*Nicole M. Speulda*

*In the following viewpoint, Trust for America's Health (TFAH)*
*contends that state and federal governments are not prepared to*
*respond to a bioterrorist attack. TFAH assessed the bioterrorism*
*response capabilities of each of the fifty states. In spite of im-*
*provements made since 2001, TFAH says the public health sys-*
*tem in most states would be overwhelmed if a bioterrorist attack*
*were to occur today. Public health facilities do not have the ca-*
*pacity or the electronic infrastructure to respond to an attack,*
*and there is a shortage of nurses and lab scientists. The organi-*
*zation offers five recommendations, including increasing govern-*
*ment accountability and modernizing technology and equip-*
*ment, to improve bioterrorism preparedness. Trust for America's*

Jeffrey Levi, Laura M. Segal, Emily Gandola, Chrissie Juliano, Nicole M. Speulda,
"Ready or Not? Protecting the Public's Health From Diseases, Disasters, and Bioterrorism," *Trust for America's Health*, December, 2006, pp. 1–63. Reproduced by permission.

*Health (TFAH) is a nonprofit organization that works to improve the health status of Americans by making disease prevention a national priority.*

As you read, consider the following questions:

1. According to Trust for America's Health (TFAH), under the U.S. Constitution, who has legal jurisdiction and responsibility for the health of its citizens?
2. According to TFAH, public health laboratories are responsible for what?
3. How much additional funding does the Public Health Foundation estimate is needed to reach minimum preparedness requirements?

2006 marks the fifth anniversary of the September 11, 2001 and anthrax tragedies. Since 2001, the nation has experienced many additional threats to the public's health, ranging from Hurricane Katrina to a life-threatening E. coli outbreak to rising concerns about a potential flu pandemic.

America's public health system and the healthcare delivery system are among the most important components of the nation's preparedness against terrorism and natural disasters. They are charged with the unique responsibility of protecting the health of all citizens. Public health and healthcare professionals act as first responders, investigators, strategists, medical care providers, and advisors to public officials and decision makers. They must diagnose and contain the spread of disease, and treat individuals who are injured or may have been exposed to infectious or harmful materials.

Intentional acts of terror and naturally occurring crises have the potential to cause serious harm to large portions of the American public. Decisions and actions taken by the public health system can greatly mitigate the negative impact of these threats and help protect the health and lives of the American people. Many health emergencies can also have serious global consequences, particularly infectious threats. Germs know no boundaries, so the U.S. must also remain vigilant and support the prevention and control of health threats around the world. . . .

## Assessing America's Readiness

In order to evaluate public health emergency preparedness in the states, Trust for America's Health (TFAH) has issued an annual *Ready or Not?* report, beginning in 2003. Each report assesses the level of preparedness in the states, evaluates the federal government's role and performance, and offers recommendations for improving emergency preparedness. *Ready or Not? 2006* is the fourth in the series.

In 2002, Congress passed the Public Health Security and Bioterrorism Act, allocating nearly $1 billion annually to states to bolster public health emergency preparedness. Even after this investment of almost $4 billion, the government health agencies have yet to release state-by-state information to Americans or policymakers about how prepared their communities are to respond to health threats.

TFAH issues this report to:

- Inform the public and policymakers about where the nation's public health system is making progress and where vulnerabilities remain;

- Foster greater transparency for public health preparedness programs;

- Encourage greater accountability for the spending of preparedness funds; and

- Help the nation move toward a strategic, "all-hazards" system capable of responding effectively to health threats posed by diseases, disasters, and bioterrorism. . . .

## Why Study States' Preparedness?

Each of the 50 states has primary legal jurisdiction and responsibility for the health of its citizens under the U.S. Constitution. The states differ in how they structure and deliver public health services. In some states, the public health system is centralized, and the state has direct control and supervision over local health agencies. In other states, local public health agencies developed separately from the state and are run by counties, cities, or townships, and usually report to one or more elected officials.

Each state has different strengths, weaknesses and unique challenges that impact its ability to prepare for and respond to public health emergencies. . . .

All Americans have the right to expect fundamental health protections during public health emergencies no matter where they live. Members of the public also deserve to know how prepared their states and communities are for different types of health threats, particularly when their taxpayer dollars are being spent to support preparedness efforts. Currently, Americans are not receiving the information they need to make decisions about how to protect themselves and their families in the event of public health emergencies. Also, they are not equipped with enough information to monitor and hold public officials accountable for whether or not their communities are adequately prepared. . . .

## Public Health Laboratories Need Upgrades and Staff

Public health laboratories are responsible for identifying naturally occurring and man-made health threats. Their identification and diagnosis process is crucial for developing strategies to contain the spread and facilitate the rapid treatment of diseases.

Eleven states report they do not have sufficient capacity to conduct laboratory tests during a bioterrorism emergency. In

2003, 44 states did not have sufficient bioterrorism laboratory capacity, indicating a major increase in capacity in the last three years.

Bioterrorism lab capacity includes having enough equipment and staff to safely handle "infectious agents that may cause serious or potentially lethal disease as a result of exposure" via inhalation. Labs with this capacity are designated with a bio-safety level 3 (BSL-3) rating.

The nation's public health laboratories encompass a "loose network of federal, state, and local laboratories that work in undefined collaboration with private clinical laboratories." The 2001 anthrax attacks demonstrated the need to upgrade and continue to maintain public health labs. The labs were quickly overwhelmed with samples from around the country, and were often left to conduct tests with inadequate equipment, facilities, and expert staff, leaving the nation more vulnerable and slower to respond. Response time would have been faster if lab capacity had been upgraded. . . .

Only 21 states reported having an adequate number of lab scientists to test for a potential anthrax or plague threat in 2004, and 41 states and D.C. reported having sufficient levels in 2005. So the current total number of 46 states and D.C. represents an improvement in the public health lab workforce's capabilities for biological threats. But there is a caveat: the increase can largely be attributed to cross-training of the scientists rather than to increases in the total number of staff in labs.

Public health laboratories face critical staff shortages, along with the rest of the public health system. A wider-scale emergency requiring surge capacity in which labs would be inundated with large numbers of samples would compound and exacerbate the workforce shortage. . . .

## Not All States Able to Track Diseases

The National Electronic Disease Surveillance System (NEDSS) was developed to integrate and standardize the tracking of infectious disease. It promotes standards-based, electronic reporting for more rapid, accurate, and integrated information. It is one component of an overarching Public Health Information Network (PHIN) at [the U.S. Centers for Disease Control] CDC. . . .

Delivering effective public health services depends on timely and reliable information. Health departments cannot protect people from existing or emerging health threats, such as a new disease outbreak or bioterror attack, without the right information. The lack of timely and comprehensive data can cause delays in identifying and responding to serious and mass emergency health problems. Additionally, federal, state, and local health departments and private healthcare providers must all work together to effectively track information about and respond to health threats.

While the CDC preparedness guidance does not require NEDSS compatibility, NEDSS provides a basis for national consistency and compatibility and is the predominant system that the CDC uses. It is currently one of the few data points about state preparedness activities that is collected and made publicly available by the CDC. A number of states that are not currently compatible with NEDSS have requested the resources they would need to accomplish this, but have not received them. . . .

## Nursing Shortage

Nurses are one of many sets of priority providers who are needed during health emergencies.

A study by the National Center for Health Workforce Analysis (NCHWA) in the Bureau of Health Professions of [the Health Resources and Services Administration] HRSA found that there is a shortage of registered nurses. If current trends continue, NCHWA estimates the national nursing shortage will reach more than one million full-time RNs by 2020. . . . Forty states and D.C. were found to have nursing shortages. . . .

## Public Health: Years of Neglect

The 9/11 terrorist attacks and subsequent anthrax attacks pushed public health emergency preparedness in the United States to the top of the national agenda. Concern has intensified with the feeble response to the 2005 Gulf Coast hurricanes and with the growing possibility of a pandemic caused by the H5N1 avian influenza virus.

The U.S. federal government has responded with an investment of some $5 billion during the past four years to upgrade the public health system's capacity to prevent and respond to large-scale public health emergencies, whether terrorism related or due to natural agents. Yet the federal government's call to arms on preparedness has fallen upon a system still in the process of recovering from years of neglect. Public health has traditionally been underfunded, and often ignored, by policymakers.

*Nicole Lurie, "Public Health Preparedness: An Opportunity and a Challange," Rand Review, Summer 2006.*

The nursing shortage makes it challenging for the healthcare sector to meet current service needs. This problem would be compounded during emergencies, when there would be an influx of additional patients. If healthcare staff levels are insufficient on a day-to-day basis, they will be exponentially overtaxed during a mass emergency. According to two recent studies, the shortage of public health nurses is even more extreme than for registered nurses overall. . . .

## Public Health Is Underfunded

Financial support for public health programs comes from a combination of federal, state, and local funds; the majority of funding comes from state and local governments. In 2000, state and local spending was 2.5 times the federal level, accounting for 70 percent of public health spending. According to an analysis in *Health Affairs*, the federal bioterrorism funding provided by Congress in FY 2002 and FY 2003 represented a 25 percent increase in the federal contribution to public health spending, which is expected to *marginally raise the total federal share of funding from 29 to 34 percent*. More than 95 percent of the new federal funds for public health preparedness are devoted to systems that were already broken and antiquated.

Despite flat or increased funding in most states during the most recent budget cycle, the funding falls far short of the estimated levels needed to reach an acceptable level of preparedness, according to most public health experts. For instance, the Public Health Foundation estimates an additional $10 billion is needed to reach the minimum preparedness requirements.

States do not report their public health budgets in consistent ways, and in many cases, there is little definition on a line basis for what the funds are used for. It is difficult to compare funding across states and to determine which public health needs are adequately funded or not within each state. Additionally, in some cases, the public health budget is not reported on separately from the total healthcare spending budget in the state.

TFAH's 2006 report, *Shortchanging America's Health; A State-By-State Look at How Federal Public Health Dollars Are Spent*, estimated that it would take an additional investment of about $2.6 billion to bring public health spending to a level that would address disparities across the states, bringing states that spend below the national average up to the average.

The median state spending on public health is currently only $31 per person per year. In comparison, median state spending is $689.93 per person annually for K-12 education; $215.34 for higher education; and $96.18 for corrections.

The IOM has urged HHS to collect information about public health budgets and programs at the state, local, and federal levels to better assess the nation's ability to provide critical public health services to every community.

TFAH recommends that all levels of government provide full, more consistent, and transparent information to the public about the funding of health programs and services. . . .

## Recommendations to Improve Preparedness

Five Years after 9/11, public health preparedness falls far short of what is required to protect the American people. The nation has made slow progress toward improving basic capabilities, but is nowhere near reaching adequate, let alone "optimally achievable," levels of preparedness across the 50 states and D.C.

TFAH calls for accelerating public health preparedness efforts, and urges an "all-hazards" approach to help protect against a range of possible threats, including bioterrorism, natural disasters, and a major outbreak of a new, lethal strain of the flu.

To strengthen emergency preparedness, we must focus on five key areas:

1. Accountability.

2. Leadership.

3. Surge capacity and the workforce.

4. Modernizing technology and equipment.

5. Partnering more with the public.

Little concrete information is available to the public or policymakers about public health preparedness and remaining vulnerabilities. While the CDC and HRSA have been working toward more clearly defining "performance measures," there is still not clear enough consensus about how to define and objectively determine standards for public health preparedness. The current measures focus too narrowly on process instead of outcomes or the ability to respond to wide-scale emergencies. Also, the information collected is largely based on self-reports and is only released in aggregate form, not on a state-by-state (or grantee-by-grantee) basis. Americans are not receiving the information they deserve to know about the safety of their own communities—or what standards they should hold the government accountable for.

HHS and its agencies should give the highest priority to defining measurable, "optimally achievable" basic preparedness standards. These need to be baseline requirements that all states should be held accountable for reaching, The measures should include objective assessments and be able to gauge improvements on an ongoing basis.

> The federal government has chosen to take a "partnership" approach with states and localities for setting measures and goals. While collaboration and different perspectives are important, the "leadership by consensus" approach has resulted in neither leadership nor consensus. At this point, most opinions and differences have been voiced, and it is up to the federal government to break the deadlock and establish standards for the use of federal funds. The federal government should either determine standards or empower a committee of experts to determine the standards, but provide a clear, firm deadline by when they must be completed.

TFAH calls for increased leadership and oversight of U.S. bioterror and public health preparedness. HHS needs to integrate top-level management of multiple bioterror and public health preparedness programs.

Major health emergencies overtax the health systems of affected communities. Local, state, and federal emergency medical and public health planning must integrate academic health centers, large private healthcare systems, and private community hospitals, and consider how to stockpile equipment and other resources. Additionally, there is a massive impending public health workforce shortage that must be immediately addressed.

Basic technology and tools of public health must be modernized to adequately protect the American people.

Planning efforts must do a better job of recognizing that the media, general public, business community, and other audiences will not always conform to procedures or expectations. Plans must be revised to address these challenges and contingencies.

# Periodical Bibliography

*The following articles have been selected to supplement the diverse views presented in this chapter.*

Sharon Begley      "Weaponized Hamburgers? An Attack on The Food Supply Is Hard to Execute But Could Sicken or Kill Thousands," *Newsweek*. July 16, 2007.

Luciana L. Borio and Gigi Kwik Gronvall      "Anthrax Countermeasures: Current Status and Future Needs," *Biosecurity and Bioterrorism: Biodefense Strategy, Practice, and Science*. November 2, 2005.

Ben Cooper      "Poxy Models and Rash Decisions," *Proceedings of the National Academy of Sciences*. 2006.

Robert Davis      "How Ready Are We for Bioterrorism?: Collegiate Case Study," *USAToday*. Available at www.usatodaycollege.com.

John H. Grote Jr. and John J. Fittipaldi      "Agroterrorism: Preparedness and Response Challenges for the Departments of Defense and Army," *Army Environmental Policy Institute*. May, 2007.

Brian Michael Jenkins      "True Grit: To Counter Terror, We Must Conquer Our Own Fear," *Rand Review*. Summer, 2006.

Nicole Lurie      Public Health Preparedness in the 21st Century, Testimony Presented Before the Senate Health, Education, Labor and Pensions Committee, Subcommittee on Bioterrorism and Public Health Preparedness on March 28, 2006. *RAND Corporation*, 2006.

Tara O'Toole      "Six Years After Anthrax: Are We Better Prepared to Respond to Bioterrorism?" Testimony before the U.S. Senate Committee on Homeland Security and Governmental Affairs on October 23, 2007. Available at www.upmc-biosecurity.org/.

# What Anti-Bioterrorism Policies Should the United States Have?

# Chapter Preface

In May 2007, the United States government placed a 31-year-old Atlanta lawyer with a rare form of tuberculosis (TB) under a federal order of isolation. TB, an infectious lung disease, was once the leading cause of death in the United States and still kills nearly 2 million people each year worldwide. It was thought that Andrew Speaker, the man placed under isolation, had contracted XDR-TB, an extremely dangerous and drug-resistant strain of TB. As it turned out, he had a milder, but still dangerous form of the disease. Speaker was the first person to be placed in isolation by order of the U.S. government since 1963.

In the weeks before his isolation, Speaker created controversy by traveling on several international commercial flights and potentially exposing others to XDR-TB. Speaker's saga, which was well-covered by the media, started when he learned he had TB. After that, despite recommendations not to travel, he flew to Paris and Athens for his wedding and honeymoon. While he was out of the country, his doctors received information indicating that Speaker had the XDR-TB form of the disease. The U.S. Centers for Disease Control and Prevention (CDC) located Speaker, who was in Rome at the time, and asked him to go to an Italian hospital. Fearing that he would not get proper care unless he was back in the United States, Speaker disobeyed this request and instead traveled from Rome to the Czech Republic where he boarded a plane to Canada. Once in Canada, Speaker rented a car and drove back to the United States. Meanwhile, the CDC issued a federal order of isolation and put Speaker's name on a federal alert list. Speaker should not have been able to cross the border from Canada to the United States without alerting authorities. However, the border guard waved Speaker through because he did not "look sick." Speaker's ability to travel out of the United States, throughout Europe, and then return to the United States, while harboring a potentially deadly disease, kindled bioterrorism fears and raised concerns about the adequacy of public health and homeland security laws and policies.

At Congressional committee meetings held soon after the incident, many legislators considered what could have happened if Speaker was a terrorist infected with smallpox, a deadly disease, which kills 30 percent of its victims and is easily spread by coughing and sneezing. "The patient was potentially a walking biological weapon, no less dangerous because he was determined to be married in Europe than he would have been if he were a terrorist intent on importing—or exporting—bioterrorism," said U.S. Representative Christopher Shays from Connecticut. The idea of a bio-suicide terrorist is not new. Foreign intelligence journalist Anthony Kimery reported in 2005 that al Qaeda–connected groups had discussed plans to use suicide bioterrorists or so-called "biomartyrs" to spread disease. Kimery wrote, "These plans are said to call for squads of suicide-willing terrorists who would deliberately infect themselves with a human transmittable strain of bird flu once such a strain has become a human contagion, or a human transmissible form clandestinely bio-engineered to be easily passed between humans, and then to spread the virus as widely around the world as they can by traveling on one international flight after another."

However, not everyone agrees with Kimery. James Carafano, a homeland security fellow at the Heritage Foundation believes the biomartyr scenario is unlikely. He is quoted as saying "a suicide bioterrorist killing by coughing out deadly, indestructible germs 'makes for great Tom Clancy kind of stuff' but would not create the instant panic and fear that just setting off a car bomb in Times Square would."

The Congressional meetings revealed several areas where public health and homeland security procedures failed. Senator Tom Harkin from Iowa said that the CDC needs to communicate with the Department of Homeland Security (DHS) in a timelier manner. He was dismayed that it took four days for the CDC to contact DHS about Speaker and get his name on a no-fly list. Julie Gerberding, head of the CDC, said the United States needs to be able to gain easier access to airline and ship passenger lists, even those that are not U.S.-bound. Speaker was able to avert a U.S. no-fly list when he flew to Canada. Finally, W. Ralph Basham, U.S. Commissioner of Customs and Border Protection, admitted that border agents must do a better job. He said that new regulations adopted since the incident will require a second supervisor to clear anyone through customs who is on an alert list. The consensus at the congressional meeting was that there is room for improvement in public health and homeland security laws and polices.

U.S. antiterrorism laws and policies are enacted to protect the country from a possible bioterrorist incident. Most analysts agree that the events surrounding Speaker's travels and subsequent isolation revealed inadequacies in these laws and policies. However, there is disagreement on how U.S. antibioterrorism laws should be bolstered. The authors of the viewpoints in the following chapter offer their opinions on this important topic.

| "Project BioShield will transform our ability to defend the nation."

# Project BioShield Is Necessary to Keep America Safe

*George W. Bush*

*In the following viewpoint, President George W. Bush, speaking at the signing of the bill to enact Project BioShield, praises the United States Congress for presenting him with such important legislation. Project BioShield, says Bush, sends a message to terrorists that the United States is not going to wait quietly while they plan another attack. Instead, says Bush, Project BioShield harnesses American scientific expertise to produce bioterrorism countermeasures, such as vaccines, new drugs, and medicines that will keep Americans safe and confront the challenge of bioterrorism. George W. Bush was elected to the United States Presidency in 2000 and 2004.*

As you read, consider the following questions:

1. According to President Bush, what two biological agents were found on Capitol Hill?

2. According to President Bush, Project BioShield authorizes how much money over how many years?

George W. Bush, "Remarks by the President at the Signing of S.15—Project BioShield Act of 2004," July 21, 2004. Available at www.whitehouse.gov/news/releases/2004/07/20040721-2.html.

3. President Bush says that Project BioShield transforms the nation's ability to defend against terrorism in three ways. What is the third way that Project BioShield helps the nation respond to terrorism?

On September the 11th, 2001, America saw the destruction and grief terrorists could inflict with commercial airlines turned into weapons of mass murder. Those attacks revealed the depth of our enemies' determination, but not the extent of their ambitions. We know that the terrorists seek an even deadlier technology. And if they acquire chemical, biological or nuclear weapons, we have no doubt they will use them to cause even greater harm.

## Project BioShield Legislation

The bill I am about to sign is an important element in our response to that threat. By authorizing unprecedented funding and providing new capabilities, Project BioShield will help America purchase, develop and deploy cutting-edge defenses against catastrophic attack.

This legislation represents the collective foresight and considered judgment of United States senators and members of the House of Representatives from both political parties— many of whom experienced bioterror firsthand when anthrax and ricin were found on Capitol Hill. It reflects 18 months of hard work and cooperation by many dedicated public servants in Congress and in the White House. It sends a message about our direction in the war on terror. We refuse to remain idle while modern technology might be turned against us; we will rally the great promise of American science and innovation to confront the greatest danger of our time. . . .

## Defends Nation in Three Ways

Project BioShield will transform our ability to defend the nation in three essential ways. First, Project BioShield authorizes $5.6 billion over 10 years for the government to purchase and

## Biotech Industry Needs Project BioShield

Good afternoon and thank you for the opportunity to testify before the Committee today on behalf of BIO, the Biotechnology Industry Organization. My name is Peter Young, and I am the President and Chief Executive of AlphaVax, Inc. AlphaVax is a privately held pre-revenue biotechnology company based in North Carolina that is working to develop and commercialize a vaccine technology that was originally invented in part at the US Army Medical Research Institute for Infectious Diseases. . . .

I wish to preface my general remarks by noting that if it were not for Project BioShield and the government's grant funding in this arena, my company would not be working on biodefense vaccine targets at all. We have no sales and no profit: the only money we have is money from people who believe we might be able to produce important new vaccines for diseases they are interested in. Biotechnology companies like mine have a limited amount of time, people, and money with which to show they can deliver on these expectations. If they don't deliver, they can't attract investment capital, and they die. If I were a big company with my own sales and profits, I would have a little more leeway, but I would still be critically answerable to the expectations of investors and the capital markets.

*Peter Young, Testimony to the U.S. House Energy and Commerce Committee, April 6, 2006.*

stockpile vaccines and drugs to fight anthrax, smallpox and other potential agents of bioterror. The Department of Health and Human Services (HHS) has already taken steps to purchase 75 million doses of an improved anthrax vaccine for the Strategic National Stockpile. Under Project BioShield, HHS is moving forward with plans to acquire a safer, second genera-tion smallpox vaccine, an antidote to botulinum toxin, and better treatments for exposure to chemical and radiological weapons.

Private industry plays a vital role in our biodefense efforts by taking risks to bring new treatments to the market, and we appreciate those efforts.

By acting as a willing buyer for the best new medical tech-nologies, the government ensures that our drug stockpile re-mains safe, effective and advanced. The federal government and our medical professionals are working together to meet the threat of bioterrorism—we're making the American people more secure.

## Facilitates the Development of New Drugs

Second, Project BioShield gives the government new authority to expedite research and development on the most promising and time-sensitive medicines to defend against bioterror. We will waste no time putting those new powers to use. Today, Secretary Thompson will direct the [National Institutes of Health] NIH to launch two initiatives—one to speed the de-velopment of new treatments for victims of a biological at-tack, and another to expedite development of treatments for victims of a radiological or nuclear attack. Under the old rules, grants of this kind of research often took 18 to 24 months to process. Under Project BioShield, HHS expects the process to be completed in about six months. Our goal is to translate today's promising medical research into drugs and vaccines to combat a biological attack in the future—and now we will not let bureaucratic obstacles stand in the way.

Third, Project BioShield will change the way the govern-ment authorizes and deploys medical defenses in a crisis. When I sign this bill, the Food and Drug Administration [FDA] will be able to permit rapid distribution of promising new drugs and antidotes in the most urgent circumstances.

This will allow patients to quickly receive the best available treatments in an emergency. Secretary Thompson has directed the FDA to prepare guidelines and procedures for implementing this new authority. By acting today, we are making sure we have the best medicine possible to help the victims of a biological attack.

Project BioShield is part of a broader strategy to defend America against the threat of weapons of mass destruction. Since September the 11th, we've increased funding for the Strategic National Stockpile by a factor of five, increased funding for biodefense research at NIH by a factor of 30, secured enough smallpox vaccine for every American, worked with cities on plans to deliver antibiotics and chemical antidotes in an emergency, improved the safety of our food supply, and deployed advanced environmental detectors under the Bio-Watch program to provide the earliest possible warning of a biological attack.

## America Can Meet the Challenge

The threat of bioterrorism has brought new challenges to our government, to our first responders and to our medical personnel. We are grateful for their service. Not long ago, few of these men and women could have imagined duties like monitoring the air for anthrax, or delivering antibiotics on a massive scale. Yet, this is the world as we find it; this nation refuses to let our guard down.

Tomorrow, the 9/11 Commission will issue its findings and recommendations to help prevent future terrorist attacks. I look forward to receiving the report. I will continue to work with the Congress and state and local governments to build on the homeland security improvements we have already made. Every American can be certain that their government will continue doing everything in our power to prevent a terrorist attack. And if the terrorists do strike, we'll be better prepared to defend our people because of the good law I sign today.

"*Project BioShield may be missing the point.*"

# Project BioShield Does Not Keep Americans Any Safer

*Debora MacKenzie*

*In the following viewpoint, Debora MacKenzie contends that Project BioShield, the centerpiece of the U.S. government's defense strategy to combat bioterrorism, has not done what it was designed to do. Project BioShield was supposed to encourage pharmaceutical companies to develop medicines and vaccines that protect against biological weapons, such as anthrax and smallpox. However, MacKenzie says, the pharmaceutical industry has not responded to BioShield incentives, and BioShield leaves many other biodefense measures unaddressed. Debora MacKenzie is a science journalist. Her articles appear frequently in* New Scientist *magazine.*

As you read, consider the following questions:

1. According to MacKenzie, what company has received the biggest slice of Project BioShield funding?

Debora MacKenzie, "Biodefence Special: Fortress America?" *New Scientist Magazine*, October 6, 2006. Reproduced by permission. Available at www.newscientist.com/special/us/mg19225725.000.

2. According to Ken Alibek, how long might it take for terrorists to engineer a more virulent or drug-resistant pathogen? How long does it typically take for researchers to develop a vaccine and have it approved?

3. According to MacKenzie, what happened after 1976 that illustrates the point that vaccines carry some risk?

It was the nightmare many had been expecting. Five years ago, hard on the heels of 9/11, someone sent anthrax spores through the US mail to journalists and politicians. Five people died, and at least 17 more got sick. The culprit was never caught.

## Massive Government Spending, But Americans No Safer

This relatively unsophisticated attack confirmed fears, already growing in the US, that with a bit more effort a determined bioterrorist could spread disease and mayhem across the nation. To combat the threat, the Bush administration launched an unprecedented biodefence effort. [As of October 2006] it has spent $44 billion—three-quarters of it aimed at protecting civilians—on new organisations, training, and buying existing remedies such as the classic smallpox vaccine.

Has this massive spending made Americans any safer? According to experts at the Center for Biosecurity at the University of Pittsburgh, the answer is no. Last month, they announced that the US remains unable to defend itself against any anthrax attack involving more than a few envelopes. So what has gone wrong?

## Project BioShield Has Ill-Advised Focus

The centrepiece of the administration's biodefence effort is Project BioShield. Launched in 2004, it is designed to turn drug companies into defence contractors, delivering products to counter potential bioweapons. Project BioShield has $5.6

billion to spend by 2014 on drugs to be stored in what is known as the Strategic National Stockpile. Yet, contrary to expectations, the pharmaceutical industry has not beaten a path to Project BioShield's door. The sluggish response has prompted a bill in Congress. . . . that attempts to make Bio-Shield more industry friendly.

Yet many biosecurity specialists say these adjustments do nothing to alter the fact that Project BioShield may be missing the point. They see problems in two crucial areas: the limited range of pathogens that BioShield is targeting, and inadequate plans for deploying the countermeasures it does have.

On the face of it, BioShield's underlying strategy seems sensible. Normally companies don't make remedies for the rare diseases thought most likely to be used as weapons, as there is no profit in it. So BioShield promises companies that it will buy particular drugs and vaccines for the threats it fears most, in theory giving the companies an incentive to do the rest.

## Industry Has Not Responded

Why, then, has the response so far has been so unimpressive? Project BioShield has awarded contracts for seven products, worth $2 billion. Two are for antibody-based therapies for botulism and anthrax. One is for 10 million doses of the military's existing anthrax vaccine—a concoction of bacterial debris whose alleged side effects have led some soldiers to prefer court-martial to vaccination. The single biggest slice of funding, $878 million, has been pledged to VaxGen of Brisbane, California, for 75 million doses of a purer, new-generation anthrax vaccine. An order is also expected for 20 million doses of an improved smallpox vaccine from the Danish firm Bavarian Nordic, while Project BioShield has provided $4 million to universities to fund basic pathogen research.

This is new territory for a government agency, which may explain the slow start. "The government has never done anything like this before," says Brad Smith of the Center for Biosecurity. The Department of Homeland Security must first decide what "designated threats" to target—and then the Department of Health commissions drugs or vaccines designed to protect against them. So far the diseases it has picked extend to anthrax, botulism and smallpox.

## One Bug, One Drug Is Flawed Approach

This targeted "one bug, one drug" approach is, however, seen by some biodefence specialists as fundamentally misguided. Ken Alibek, head of the Soviet and then Russian bacterial weapons programme until 1992, says it allows attackers to create pathogens that evade or resist each remedy as fast as it is developed. "Based on the former Soviet model, it takes three to four years to engineer a drug-resistant or more virulent pathogen," he says. "It takes 10 to 15 years to develop a vaccine and have it approved." Jonathan Tucker of the Center for Nonproliferation Studies, a think tank in Washington DC, agrees. "It is myopic to focus on the designated threat organisms," he says, "especially when the bigger threat is probably from natural disease."

A better approach, these critics say, would be to aim for broad-spectrum remedies that work against many different bacteria or viruses. That would be more cost-effective, offer a blanket defence against terrorists whatever their choice of bioweapon, and come with the huge additional benefit of protecting against natural diseases too. "If something works for flu and for bioweapons as well, why not do that?" says Tucker.

BioShield has not pursued broad-spectrum remedies, partly because it is not allowed to fund anything that might be profitable in its own right. But according to Tucker, drug firms aren't making broad-spectrum antivirals precisely because they don't see them as profitable. "This is the sort of market failure that governments are supposed to step in and remedy if it is in the public interest," he says.

The Department of Defense, which provides biodefence for soldiers rather than civilians, seems less inhibited. This year it started awarding research grants under the new Transformational Medical Technologies Initiative, which aims to attack the common structures and functions of pathogens. That should lead to remedies effective against many organisms, including emerging diseases or genetically modified bioweapons.

James Joyce of Aethlon Medical in San Diego, California, which makes a device that removes viruses from blood, hopes this signals a new direction for Project BioShield. "The DoD's recent shift to broad-spectrum post-exposure therapeutics will set the tone for changes in BioShield, or perhaps new legislation," he says. Some companies already involved in BioShield seem to agree. PharmAthene is merging with Siga Technologies, based in New York City, which is developing broad-spectrum antibacterials as well as a promising smallpox drug.

## BioShield Does Not Address Vaccine Delivery Issues

Whatever countermeasures are developed, they will be pointless unless they can be delivered in a timely and effective way. This is the second area where critics say Project BioShield falls short. While the federal government buys and stockpiles biodefence remedies, more than 3000 separate state, city and tribal administrations are expected to deliver them to the US population in an emergency, and the public health agencies they rely on to do the job have been underfunded for decades. The chaotic response to hurricane Katrina [in 2005] showed how easily state and local resources can be overwhelmed in the absence of help from Washington.

The Center for Biosecurity estimates that state public health departments have received an extra $4 billion since 2001 to equip labs and hire epidemiologists and "bioterrorism

## Frivolous and Unnecessary

In a momentary glance, Project BioShield appears to be an effective and valuable response to the looming fear of a biological or chemical weapons attack. However, when analyzing the Act with greater scrutiny, the negative points and unrealistic intentions are prominent. For example, the expedited approval of drugs through the Food and Drug Administration ("FDA"), which empowers the FDA with unprecedented authority. Moreover, legislators believe that Project BioShield is a frivolous unnecessary law. The [U.S. Congressman] Honorable Jeff Flake stated:

> This legislation is another example of the federal government attempting to throw money at a project that is already underway. The Department of Health and Human Services already administers the Strategic National Stockpile, which combat the public health consequences of a terrorist attack or public health emergencies. The Department of Homeland Security currently provides the financing for those efforts ... About $400 million was appropriated in 2003 for stockpiling activities.

*Jodi Phillipo, "Project BioShield: More Than Meets the Eye,"*
*Berkeley Electronic Press. 2005.*

coordinators". Similar amounts have gone to hospitals and local governments for bioterrorism "preparedness". Despite this it says hospitals' capacity to absorb an unexpected surge of patients from an attack—or an epidemic—has not improved, because relatively little money has been spent on that aspect.

Research by Tucker and Andrew Grotto of the Center for American Progress, another Washington DC think tank, shows far more effort is required. "Only seven states and four cities have the capability to administer stockpiled vaccines on a large scale," Tucker says. More than half of all Americans live in states that have no plans for dealing with large numbers of casualties from any cause, he adds, and only two states have plans for encouraging medical personnel to report for work during an outbreak of contagious disease.

The bill before Congress attempts to address some of these problems. It creates a new assistant health secretary for public health, improves planning and equipment for medical emergencies, and provides $1 billion a year funding. But this may not be enough to solve the delivery problem, or give hospitals the capacity to deal with a surge in patients.

## Need Corps of Vaccinated First-Responders

An additional problem is that most vaccines have to be given well before any outbreak or bio-attack. Yet vaccinating the general population against every likely bioterror agent is a prohibitively expensive non-starter, Alibek says. So vaccines developed under BioShield—one for Ebola is likely—would probably only be used after an attack, to keep the disease from spreading to uninfected people. That means planning in advance where to go and who to vaccinate, and having enough people on the ground to do it—preferably people who are themselves vaccinated. None of these conditions is met by any of the US's overburdened public health agencies, for any of the diseases considered the most likely to be exploited in a bio-attack. An effort to create such a corps of responders by vaccinating healthcare workers against smallpox failed in 2003.

Any vaccine also carries some risk, however small, of side effects. If a vaccination drive were to be launched against a threat that failed to materialise, people who suffered side effects might feel they had been damaged needlessly, and sue the vaccine maker. That happened after 1976 when thousands of Americans were vaccinated against a swine flu epidemic that never occurred.

With this in mind, [in 2005] Congress made a last-minute addition to a big defence bill that would require anyone filing a lawsuit against manufacturers of biodefence medications to prove deliberate negligence—a more stringent test than for most such suits. To make up for this, the law also introduced an entitlement to compensation for people damaged by such products. What it has not done, however, is set aside money for the compensation fund, and that, Tucker says, could discourage people from accepting BioShield treatments.

All is not lost. . . . Congress [is considering legislation that] mandates research into new tools and methods for developing drugs and vaccines, not just the drugs and vaccines themselves. That may go some way to moving Project BioShield's focus away from the "one bug, one drug" strategy and on to a broader spectrum of remedies. But it does little to solve the problems of how to get any remedies out to the potential victims of a bioweapons attack. Nor does it mandate stronger safety trials that might help identify side effects of any new therapies, and so give the public a better idea of the risks and benefits of the drugs and vaccines on offer. For now, the authorities appear bent on building a stockpile of silver bullets against imagined enemies that may not work or may never be needed.

*"Passage of S.3678 [the Pandemic and All-Hazards Preparedness Act] marks a major milestone in improving public health and hospital preparedness for bioterrorist attacks."*

# The Pandemic and All-Hazards Preparedness Act Helps Protects Against Bioterrorism

*Michael Mair, Beth Maldin, and Brad Smith*

*In the following viewpoint, Michael Mair, Beth Maldin, and Brad Smith, of the Center for Biosecurity, claim that the Pandemic and All-Hazards Preparedness Act will protect Americans against bioterrorism by improving public health and hospital infrastructure. The authors point out the highlights of the legislation, noting that it provides for electronic disease reporting, strengthens the Military Reserve Corps (MRC) program, and establishes the Biomedical Advanced Research and Development Authority (BARDA) to facilitate the development of new medicines and vaccines that can be used against bioterrorism. The*

Michael Mair, Beth Maldin, and Brad Smith, "Passage of S. 3678: The Pandemic and All-Hazards Preparedness Act", *Center for Biosecurity, University of Pittsburgh Medical Center*, December 20, 2006. Reproduced by permission. Available at www.upmc biosecurity.org/website/focus/public_health_prep/2006-12-20-allhazardsprepact.pdf.

*Pandemic and All-Hazards Preparedness Act became a public law on December 19, 2006. The Center for Biosecurity is a non-profit organization that works to affect policy and practice in ways that lessen the impacts of bioterrorism and pandemic outbreaks.*

As you read, consider the following questions:

1. What does ESAR VHP stand for?
2. According to the authors, how often does the secretary for the Department of Health and Human Services have to prepare and submit to Congress a report on the National Health Security Strategy for coordinated public health?
3. The Biodefense Medical Counter Measures Development Fund allows BARDA to fund the development of products across the so-called Valley of Death. What does the "Valley of Death" refer to?

On December 19, 2006, President Bush signed the Pandemic and All-Hazards Preparedness Act (S. 3678) into law. Passage of S. 3678 marks a major milestone in improving public health and hospital preparedness for bioterrorist attacks, pandemics, and other catastrophes and for improving the development of new medical countermeasures, such as medicines and vaccines, against biosecurity threats. Highlights of the legislation's key initiatives are summarized below.

## National Preparedness and Response, Leadership, Organization, and Planning

1. Creates the Assistant Secretary for Preparedness and Response within the Department of Health and Human Services (HHS) and consolidates the responsibilities for federal public health and medical emergency preparedness and response activities under that office. This includes authority over the National Disaster Medical Sys-

tem (NDMS) and the Hospital Preparedness Cooperative Agreement Program, the coordination of the Medical Reserve Corps (MRC), the Emergency System for Advance Registration of Volunteer Health Professional (ESAR VHP), the Strategic National Stockpile (SNS), and the Cities Readiness Initiative (CRI). The Assistant Secretary will oversee advanced research, development, and procurement of "qualified countermeasures" and "qualified pandemic or epidemic products." The Assistant Secretary will be nominated by the President and confirmed by the Senate.

2. Requires the Secretary of HHS to appoint an official who will provide guidance to public health agencies on incorporating the needs of at-risk individuals in federal, state, and local preparedness and response strategies. This appointee will ensure that the SNS addresses the needs of at-risk populations (including non-pharmaceutical supplies), will oversee development of curriculum for training programs on medical management of at-risk individuals, and will disseminate best practices for outreach to and care for at-risk individuals before, during, and following public health emergencies.

3. Requires the Secretary to prepare and submit to Congress the National Health Security Strategy for coordinated public health preparedness and response. This will begin in 2009 and will be prepared every 4 years thereafter. The strategy will include evaluation of federal, state, local, and tribal progress measured according to evidence-based benchmarks.

## Public Health Security Preparedness

1. Provides for cooperative agreements (i.e., grants) to state and select local public health entities to improve health security. Funding will be contingent on a number of requirements. For example, eligible entities must submit

an application "containing such information as the Secretary may require," including a plan for entities to obtain public comment and input on preparedness and response plans. In addition, beginning in FY 2009, states must participate in ESAR VHP to qualify for funding. In making awards, the Secretary of [the Department of Health and Human Services] HHS must consult with the Secretary of the Department of Homeland Security (DHS) to ensure maximum coordination with the Metropolitan Medical Response System (MMRS), minimize redundant funding of programs, develop recommendations and guidance on best practices, and disseminate information about lessons learned through a single internet site.

2. Requires non-federal contributions to public health preparedness programs. Beginning in 2009, the Secretary may not award a cooperative agreement unless a state, or a consortium of two or more states, agrees that it will make non-federal contributions available to public health preparedness programs. States may disburse funds directly, or funds may be provided through donations from public or private entities. The funding may be provided in cash or in kind. For the first fiscal year of the cooperative agreement, the state must provide at least 5% of the funding, and from the second fiscal year on, the state must provide at least 10% of the funding. Entities that receive cooperative agreements must have their expenditures independently audited at least every two years, and the audit report must be submitted to the Secretary within 30 days of the audit's completion.

3. Requires the Secretary—in consultation with state, local, and tribal officials as well as private entities—to develop or adopt measurable, evidence-based benchmarks to gauge preparedness. Entities that do not meet bench-

mark requirements will have the opportunity to correct non-compliance. Beginning in FY 2009, the Secretary shall withhold funds from each entity that has failed substantially to meet benchmarks or has failed to submit a pandemic influenza plan.

4. Authorizes the Secretary to award grants entities such as hospitals, clinical laboratories, and universities for improvements in real-time disease detection. This funding is for programs to purchase and implement advanced diagnostic medical equipment to analyze clinical specimens in real-time to determine the presence of pathogens of public health and/or bioterrorism significance.

5. Requires the Secretary to establish a nationwide, near real-time electronic public health situational awareness capability. This capability will be established in collaboration with state, local, and tribal public health authorities and will provide for the secure sharing of critical public health and medical information. The legislation stipulates that this capability be accomplished "through an interoperable network of systems. . .built on existing State situational awareness systems or enhanced systems that enable such connectivity." Grants may be awarded to states or consortia of states, to support implementation of the network of situational awareness systems. No later than 4 years following enactment, [Government Accountability Office] GAO will conduct an independent evaluation of this effort and submit to the Secretary and Congress a progress report.

6. Authorizes the Secretary to provide grants to states for tuition loan repayment to individuals who agree to serve for at least 2 years in state, local, or tribal health departments. The loan repayment program will support degree programs appropriate for serving in state, local, and tribal health departments.

7. Authorizes the Secretary to cooperate with manufacturers, wholesalers, and distributors during a pandemic on tracking initial distribution of federally purchased influenza vaccine. In addition, the law requires that the Secretary promote communication among state, local, and tribal public health officials and manufactures, wholesalers, and distributors regarding the effective distribution of seasonal influenza vaccine to high priority populations during vaccine shortages and supply disruptions.

## All-Hazards Medical Surge Capacity

1. Transfers NDMS functions, personnel, assets, and liabilities from the Department of Homeland Security to the Department of Health and Human Services.

2. Strengthens federal support and structure for the Medical Reserve Corps (MRC) program, beginning with the appointment of a Director by the Secretary. The Director will be responsible for overseeing activities of state, local, and tribal corps chapters. This legislation aims to establish, through the ESAR VHP, an interoperable network of connected state systems to verify the credentials and licenses of healthcare professionals who volunteer during public health emergencies. This will be accessible to all local and state health departments.

3. Expands the Epidemic Intelligence Service Program. Managed by [the Centers for Disease and Control] CDC, the Epidemic Intelligence Service (EIS) is a 2-year postgraduate program of service and on-the-job training for health professionals interested in epidemiology. This legislation creates an additional 20 EIS officer positions. Individuals work for at least 2 years at a state, local, or tribal health department that serves an area in which there is a shortage of health professionals, a medically underserved population, or a high risk of public health emergency.

## Important Board Created

U.S. Senator Richard Burr today praised the formation of the National Biodefense Science Board, which will advise the U.S. Secretary of Health and Human Services (HHS) on trends, challenges, and opportunities presented by advances in biological and life sciences, including naturally occurring infectious diseases and chemical, biological, radiological or nuclear agents. The board was authorized by Burr's *Pandemic and All-Hazards Preparedness Act* (P.L. 109-417), which was signed into law in December of last year.

"The creation of this board is a critical step forward in preparing the country for future threats to public health, such as bioterror agents or evolving flu viruses," Burr said. "This group will play a central role in ensuring our government identifies new and emerging threats as well as opportunities for innovation to prevent, prepare, and respond to those threats. By seeking advice and guidance from the best scientists and engineers in the country, the federal government is taking the lead in keeping Americans safe."

*Richard Burn, Senate Press Release, June 19, 2007.*

4. Requires the Secretary to award grants to hospital and healthcare facilities to improve surge capacity and enhance community and hospital preparedness for public health emergencies.

## Pandemic and Biodefense Vaccine and Drug Development

1. Requires the development of a Strategic Plan for Countermeasure Research, Development, and Procurement. The Secretary of HHS is directed to develop a strategic plan, within 6 months of enactment, that "integrates biodefense and emerging infectious disease requirements with . . . advanced research

and development, strategic initiatives for innovation, and the procurement of [countermeasure and pandemic] products."

## BARDA

2. Establishes the Biomedical Advanced Research and Development Authority (BARDA). Operating within HHS, BARDA will facilitate the development of new medicines and vaccines (i.e., medical countermeasures) to counter biological, chemical, radiological, nuclear, and other security threats. A Director will be appointed by the Secretary.

BARDA's mission:

- Facilitate collaboration among the U.S. government, relevant biopharma companies, and academic researchers to develop medical countermeasures.

- Support the "advanced research and development" of medical countermeasures through contracts, prizes, and other means (see below).

- Promote "innovation to reduce the time and cost of countermeasure . . . development" as well as to improve the development of research tools, rapid diagnostics, broad spectrum anti-microbials, and vaccine technologies (see below). BARDA is exempt from certain Freedom of Information Act (FOIA) disclosure requirements for information that "reveals significant and not otherwise publicly known vulnerabilities of existing medical or public health defenses." This exemption is subject to review every 5 years by the Secretary, and will sunset after 7 years.

3. Establishes the "Biodefense Medical Countermeasure Development Fund" to allow BARDA to fund the development of products across the so-called "Valley of Death" between NIH-funded basic research and end-stage procurement by the BioShield program. The law authorizes $1.07 billion for

FY 2006–2008 for the fund. This Fund is separate from the preexisting BioShield purchase fund. This fund may also be used to support innovation in biomedical research tools and other strategic initiatives intended to improve overall medical countermeasure development.

4. Establishes the National Biodefense Science Board. The board will "provide expert advice and guidance to the Secretary on scientific, technical, and other matters . . . regarding current and future chemical, biological, nuclear, and radiological agents, whether naturally occurring, accidental, or deliberate." The board will consist of U.S. government officials, 4 representatives of the biopharma and medical device industry, 4 academic representatives, and 5 others including at least one practicing healthcare professional and one representative of healthcare consumers.

5. Directs the [Food and Drug Administration] FDA to provide technical assistance to the developers of medical countermeasures on manufacturing and regulatory processes.

6. Establishes limited anti-trust exemptions to allow biopharma companies to better collaborate with each other and with government in the development of medical countermeasures. This provision will sunset after 6 years.

7. Makes reforms to the BioShield procurement program which was established in 2004:

- Confers authority to HHS for making multiple milestone-based advanced payments of 5% of the total contract (up to 50% of the total contract).

- Gives HHS the authority to contract for domestic "warm base surge capacity" for a developer to establish a warm base manufacturing capacity for a countermeasure that may be brought on-line quickly (e.g., during a crisis).

- Allows HHS to enter into an exclusive contract with a vendor.

> "BARDA will essentially be accountable to nobody and can operate without having to worry about troublesome interference from courts or private citizens like you and me."

# The Pandemic and All-Hazards Preparedness Act Has Troubling Secrecy Provisions

## OMB Watch

*In the following viewpoint, OMB Watch raises concerns about exemptions from the Freedom of Information Act (FOIA) given to the Biomedical Advanced Research and Development Agency (BARDA) under legislation introduced by Senator Richard Burr in 2005. The legislation was never enacted. However, BARDA was established and granted some secrecy provisions in other legislation before the U.S. Congress. OMB Watch disapproves of the exemptions, saying that all areas of government must remain accountable to the public. OMB Watch is a nonprofit research and advocacy organization dedicated to promoting government accountability and regulatory policy to serve the public interest.*

OMB Watch, "A New Ultra-Secret Government Agency," *OMB Watch*, November 29, 2005. Reproduced by permission. Available at www.ombwatch.org/article/articleview/3195/1/404.

As you read, consider the following questions:

1. According to OMB Watch, do the CIA and the Department of Defense have an exemption similar to the one given to BARDA?

2. According to OMB Watch, what are government agencies compelled to do when the public requests agency records?

3. According to OMB Watch, what does the Federal Advisory Committee Act require?

Legislation [has been] in the [U.S.] Senate [that would] create a new government agency to combat bioterrorism that [would] operate, unlike any other agency before it, under blanket secrecy protection.

Sen. Richard Burr introduced the Biodefense and Pandemic Vaccine and Drug Development Act of 2005, S1873, that would create a new agency in the Department of Health and Human Services (HHS) to research and develop strategies to combat bioterrorism and natural diseases. While Congress has created several agencies recently in response to homeland security concerns, most notably the Department of Homeland Security, Burr proposes for the first time ever to completely exempt this new agency from all open government laws.

## Blanket FOIA Exemption for BARDA

The Act creates the Biomedical Advanced Research and Development Agency (BARDA) to work on countering bioterrorism and natural diseases. Apparently in an attempt to protect any and all sensitive information on U.S. counter-bioterrorism efforts or vulnerabilities to biological threats, Burr has included in the legislation the first-ever blanket exemption from the Freedom of Information Act (FOIA). The legislation states that, "Information that relates to the activities, working groups, and advisory boards of the BARDA shall not be subject to disclosure" under FOIA "unless the Secretary [of HHS] or Direc-

## Public's Right to Know Suffers

The biggest casualty of a conflict between scientists and security agencies may be open research institutions and the public's right to know about dangerous experiments with biological weapons agents. With proposed new secrecy, lab accountability will diminish, leading to more accidents, poor judgment, and a decline of international confidence in US biodefense research.

In a proposed law on the Senate floor, a giant new biodefense "sensitive but unclassified" (SBU) hole would be torn in the Freedom of Information Act, creating new secrecy at labs across the country. It is a ham fisted attempt to resolve conflicts between secretive spies and cocky scientists who disagree over risks posed by research on biological weapons agents.

*Sunshine Project News Release, February 7, 2006*

tor [of BARDA] determines that such disclosure would pose no threat to national security."

Neither the CIA nor the Defense Department has such an exemption. Burr's spokesperson argues that the exemption is necessary to protect national security claiming that "there will be times where for national security reasons certain information would have to be withheld." For instance, the BARDA should not, according to the spokesperson, be required to publicly disclose information pertaining to a deadly virus.

## No Reason for Exemption

FOIA, however, already includes an exemption for national security information, as well as eight other exemptions ranging from privacy issues to confidential business information and law enforcement investigations. If the public disclosure of information would threaten national security, then the government may withhold the requested information. "The well-established and time-tested FOIA provisions already address Burr's concerns," explains Sean Moulton, OMB Watch senior policy analyst, "thereby making the blanket exemption for BARDA unnecessary and unwise."

Congress established and strengthened FOIA over the years to create a reasonable, consistent level of accountability among government agencies. Under FOIA, when the public requests agency records, the agency is compelled to collect and review the requested information. The only decision for the agency is whether specific records can or can not be released under the law based on the exemptions from disclosure written into the law. However, the Burr legislation reverses the process: it does not require BARDA to collect or review the requests for disclosure. Instead, the agency can automatically reject requests. Still more troubling, the law prohibits any challenges of determinations by the Director of BARDA or Secretary of HHS, stating that the determination of the Director or Secretary with regards to the decision to withhold information "shall not be subject to judicial review."

Mark Tapscott at the Heritage Foundation writes that "BARDA will essentially be accountable to nobody and can operate without having to worry about troublesome interference from courts or private citizens like you and me."

This move to restrict the reach of FOIA appears in stark contrast to the recent Senate vote to strengthen open government. Sens. John Cornyn (R-TX) and Patrick Leahy (D-VT) co-sponsored FOIA reform legislation, passed by the Senate in June 2005, that "will bring additional sunshine to the federal legislative process, and was another step toward strengthening the Freedom of Information Act."

## Public Prevented from Knowing Whether BARDA Works

The Biodefense and Pandemic Vaccine and Drug Development Act also exempts BARDA from important parts of the Federal Advisory Committee Act, which requires public disclosure of advice given to the executive branch by advisory, committees, task forces, boards and commissions.

Other provisions of the bill compound the troubling secrecy provisions. They include:

- Giving BARDA the authority to sign exclusive contracts with drug manufacturers and forbidding the agency from purchasing generic versions of these drugs or vaccines.

- Authorizing BARDA to issue grants and rebates for drug companies to produce vaccines.

- Providing liability protection to drug manufacturers for drugs and vaccines not approved by the Food and Drug Administration, by requiring the secretary of HHS find that a drug company willfully caused injury.

The FOIA exemption in combination with these provisions would prevent the public from knowing whether BARDA is effectively completing these duties. Only information on agency actions could establish if the new agency is protecting the public from bioterrorism and infectious disease or if it is simply providing handouts to drug companies that creates no added security.

## We Must Hold Government Accountable

"It is essential that open government safeguards remain in place for all agencies," Moulton continues. "It is extremely important to ensure that the nation is protected against pandemics and bioterrorist attacks, but such efforts must not be excluded from open government. By providing the mechanisms for government accountability, these safeguards ensure that the government meets its responsibility to protect the public. In the end, an accountable government is a stronger government which acts to effectively meet all threats, including pandemics and bioterrorism."

> *"The consequences of refusing anthrax vaccine include that service members will be more vulnerable to lethal anthrax infection."*

# The Anthrax Vaccine Is Safe and Protects Military Personnel

*Military Vaccine (MILVAX) Agency*

*In the following viewpoint, the Military Vaccine (MILVAX) Agency of the U.S. Department of Defense (DoD) asserts that the anthrax vaccine the military uses to vaccinate soldiers is safe, effective, and crucial for protecting soldiers' lives and carrying out a successful mission. MILVAX says that anthrax poses a real threat, particularly to service members in harm's way. Soldiers have the right to refuse the vaccine. But, says MILVAX, in doing so, they could be jeopardizing their lives, the lives of others in their unit, and the success of the mission. Note: On October 2006, the DoD eliminated the option to refuse the anthrax vaccine and began requiring anthrax vaccinations for all service members. The MILVAX Agency is the lead agency responsible for disseminating information about DoD immunization policies.*

Department of Defense Anthrax Immunization Program Information (Anthrax.MIL), December 19, 2005. Available at www.anthrax.mil/documents/864Dec2005house inhouse-out.pdf.

As you read, consider the following questions:

1. What is the name of the spore-forming bacteria that causes anthrax?

2. According to MILVAX, what is the rate of side effects away from the injection site, and what percentage of vaccine recipients experience these side effects?

3. What data is provided to show that anthrax vaccination does not increase the risk of disability?

Anthrax is a robust spore-forming bacterium (*Bacillus anthracis*) that can be stored for years, loaded into a variety of weapons, and produced in large quantities without sophisticated equipment. Inhalation anthrax is 99% lethal in an unprotected, unvaccinated population, left untreated.

## Anthrax Poses Real Threat

- The threat is real and failure to prepare would result in grave consequences. A former Director of the Central Intelligence Agency, James Woolsey, referred to it as "the single most dangerous threat to our national security in the foreseeable future."

- Several countries have or are developing an offensive biological warfare capability using anthrax.

- Anthrax is a deadly infection. In the fall of 2001, 22 cases of anthrax resulted from attacks with anthrax spores. Five people died in these attacks.

- Iraq conducted weapons tests in 1990; biological warfare bombs and warheads were moved to forward locations during the Gulf War: thousands of pounds of anthrax spores were loaded into missiles, aerial bombs, and spray tanks.

- Admissions in the post-Cold War era of the former Soviet Union's massive biological warfare capability confirmed their anthrax and smallpox programs were highly developed.

## Vaccine Is Safe, Refusing It Is Risky

To prevent an anthrax infection, anthrax vaccine is the safest means of protection for high risk personnel. After an anthrax attack, antibiotics would be given to increase survival even further. Antibiotics plus vaccination would be given to get survival as close to 100% as possible. Nonetheless, anthrax vaccine is the best round-the-clock protection available.

Military services will continue anthrax vaccinations as they have since April 2005, with the same people eligible and the same option to refuse, until [the Department of Defense] DoD completes its review of the [Food and Drug Administration] FDA's Final Order. As with the [Emergency Use Authorization] EUA, if vaccination is refused, no disciplinary action or adverse personnel action will be taken. They will not be processed for separation, and they will still be deployable.

The consequences of refusing anthrax vaccine include that service members will be more vulnerable to lethal anthrax infection. Their loss could threaten the lives of others in their unit who depend on them, and could jeopardize the success of the mission.

The issue of mandatory vaccination will be reconsidered after further review of the FDA's Final Order.

## Anthrax Vaccine Is Effective

Field studies conducted in the 1950s by Centers for Disease Control researchers demonstrated more than 92 percent vaccine effectiveness in humans (jointly against cutaneous and inhalational anthrax).

The Food and Drug Administration licensed anthrax vaccine as a safe and effective prevention against *Bacillus anthra-*

*cis*—the bacteria causing anthrax. The FDA reaffirmed this position to Congressional committees over multiple years, including a December 15, 2005, Final Order stating that anthrax vaccine prevents anthrax resulting from any route of exposure, including inhalation. Based on human and animal data, the National Academy of Sciences' Institute of Medicine concluded in March 2002 that anthrax vaccine is "an effective vaccine for the protection of humans against anthrax, including inhalational anthrax."

Animal studies consistently demonstrate protection—non-human primates with only one or two vaccinations survived lethal challenges with many times over the median lethal dose (LD50) up to 2 years later. In all, 62 of 65 vaccinated monkeys (95 percent) survived inhalation challenge, but 0 of 18 unvaccinated monkeys (0 percent) survived. Similarly, 114 of 117 vaccinated rabbits survived, but unvaccinated rabbits died. Correlates of immunity that allow comparisons from animals to humans have not been fully developed. . . .

## Anthrax Vaccine Is as Safe as Others

- 20 safety studies of more than 800,000 vaccine recipients establish the safety of anthrax vaccine. This vaccine has been used for over 35 years.

- As with any vaccine, injection-site reactions do occur. Mild injection-site reactions, such as redness, swelling, and tenderness (less than one inch), occur in up to 30 percent of men and 60 percent of women. About 1 in 100 develops a reaction five inches or larger. Such symptoms resolve on their own in a few days.

- The rate of side effects away from the injection site—fatigue, headache, muscle or joint pain—occur in 5% to 35% of vaccine recipients; again, they typically resolve within 24 to 48 hours. As the National Academy of Sciences noted in their March 2002 report, these rates are similar to other vaccines.

## As Protected as You Can Be

"Imagine a very slowly descending escalator that you're climbing," said Army Capt. Remington Nevin, preventive medicine physician, Combined Joint Task Force-82. "Once you've completed your six dosage series you are as protected as you can be at the top of the escalator."

Nevin's analogy describes the recent [Central Command] CENTCOM policy mandating all servicemembers working in the CENTCOM area of operations for 15 or more consecutive days receive an anthrax vaccination. This mandatory vaccination extends to key Department of Defense contractors and certain civilian employees.

*Timothy Dinneen,*
*"Anthrax Vaccine To Be Mandatory for Centcom,"*
Defend America, *May 14, 2007.*

- If a service member has a serious reaction to anthrax vaccine, he/she will be exempted from further doses and will receive full medical care. This policy is the same as for any vaccination.

- Anthrax vaccine is as safe as other vaccines. Multi-year studies found no patterns of long-term health problems due to anthrax vaccination. A vaccine, like any medicine, could possibly cause serious problems. The risk of anthrax vaccine causing serious harm, or death, is extremely small.

- The National Academy of Sciences' Institute of Medicine reported in March 2002, "There is no evidence that life-threatening or permanently disabling immediate-onset adverse events occur at higher rates in individuals who have received AVA [U.S. anthrax vaccine] than in the general population." In rare cases, patients experience serious adverse effects; these are treated and followed appropriately.

• Between March 1998 and Dec 2005, more than 1.3 million people have been vaccinated against anthrax.

• The anthrax vaccine was invented using mid-century technology that also led to highly successful vaccines against influenza, tetanus, diphtheria, and other infectious diseases.

• The license to manufacture anthrax vaccine has been valid without interruption since 1970. BioPort's [the manufacturer of the military's vaccine] license was amended and approved by the FDA to reflect the renovated facilities and processes.

• An October 2004 review of over 716,000 active-duty service members discharge rates shows anthrax vaccination does not increase risk of disability. Overall, the disability evaluation rate in the Army was very low for the 4.25 years covered by this study, and there appeared to be no effect of exposure to anthrax vaccine on the risk of disability evaluation.

## No Vaccine Effect on Fertility or Cancer

Virtually no vaccine is studied for cancer or effects on reproductive health, largely because such problems have not previously been seen with any vaccine. Prevailing scientific knowledge, based on literally billions of vaccinations administered since 1796, is that vaccines do not cause such problems; the manufacturing process and constituents of anthrax vaccine are similar to other vaccines.

A 2005 study of male fertility found a diagnosis of male-factor infertility was less common in anthrax-vaccinated men than in unvaccinated men. Vaccination didn't impair semen parameters, fertilization rate, embryo quality or clinical pregnancy rates.

A study suggests that anthrax vaccine may be linked with birth defects if given *during* pregnancy. Pregnant women should not be vaccinated against anthrax unless the potential benefits of vaccination outweigh the potential risk.

We know from large database studies that vaccinated and unvaccinated service members have the same likelihood of cancer or fertility problems. There is no vaccine effect. . . .

## Squalene in Vaccines Is Safe

Squalene (a substance naturally produced by the human body) has never been added to anthrax vaccine. Food and Drug Administration (FDA) scientists found trace quantities of squalene in anthrax, diphtheria, and tetanus vaccines (less than the natural level of squalene in the human bloodstream). But other tests did not confirm this finding. The FDA notes that these minute quantities could have come from processing during FDA tests (squalene is present in the oil in fingerprints). The FDA called squalene in vaccines "naturally occurring and safe."

*"The shoddy actions of the military in administering the anthrax vaccine seemed to have endangered soldiers' health."*

# The U.S. Government Should Not Force the Anthrax Vaccine on Military Personnel

**Gary Null with James Feast**

*In the following viewpoint, Gary Null and James Feast contend that there are myriad problems with the anthrax vaccine the military is making its soldiers take, including how the vaccine is being administered. Null and Feast point out that the military is using an anthrax vaccine that has not been widely studied and has not been conclusively proven safe, and they are administering it with disregard to scientific protocol and dismissing soldiers' complaints. Null and Feast say there is reason to believe the anthrax vaccine is implicated in Gulf War Illness. Gary Null is a talk radio host and author on health, nutrition, and alternative medicine. James Feast is an editor of the* Journal of the History of Philosophy.

As you read, consider the following questions:

1. What is a VAERS form?

2. What is the name of the plant located in Michigan that makes the anthrax vaccine that the author notes has been suspected of some improprieties?

3. What is a Russian Doll Cocktail?

Some have argued that the best way to understand a society is to observe where things don't add up. Those areas indicate strains that will eventually cause innovation or breakdown. In the United States, there is the glaring contradiction between a respected, well-funded scientific establishment and the set of institutions, such as the political structure, that provides science's funding, and then utilizes scientific findings with a reckless disregard for the field's procedures, perspective, and ethos.

First, we will see how the shoddy actions of the military in administering the anthrax vaccine seemed to have endangered soldiers' health, then we'll look at the paucity of tests on the vaccine, which cleared it for widespread use. From there, we quickly survey the possibility the vaccine may have illness-provoking additives, that out-of-date vaccines have been administered in the past, and that the vaccine is not relevant to the type of germs that will be employed by terrorists or military enemies. We end by seeing whether the vaccine is implicated in Gulf War illnesses.

What we have in mind in relation to the first point is the situation that came about when United States troops were given anthrax vaccine, preparatory to their going into the field against Iraq. The vaccine had never been employed on such scale, having previously only occasionally been administered to those that worked with animals. Inoculating hundreds of thousands of troops presented an opportunity to test the drug's mettle.

## The Military Was in Charge

If scientists had been in control, a careful monitoring of the inoculees could have been undertaken and the drug's effects could have been rigorously assessed in hopes of working on its improvement. Instead the military was in charge. The armed forces are set up to win battles, not conduct scientific investigations. Where medical research depends on open, collegial sharing of all information in a democratic atmosphere, the military relies on cover-ups, the seclusion of knowledge from all but the higher-ups, and a hierarchical chain of command.

A study by Garth Nicolson and colleagues from the Institute for Molecular Medicine in Huntington Beach, California, and Parkview Hospital in Brunswick, Maryland, brings out some of the counter-scientific procedures indulged in when the military administered the drugs. Accepted procedure for evaluating vaccines, according to Nicolson et al., is for an independent contractor (independent from the agency providing the dosage) to evaluate the inoculated, recording *any* adverse reactions, which are then tabulated and sent to the FDA's Vaccine Adverse Event Reporting System (VAERS). "In the case of anthrax vaccine, military physicians were instructed that only certain adverse effects could be vaccine reactions. . .and others such as joint pain, cognitive disturbances, etc. could not be due to the vaccine." The military doctors had no access to data on the varied side effects recorded for the vaccine, including joint pains and others they were told not to report, nor did they look for long-term effects. The upshot was "only reactions that resulted in hospitalization or immediate loss of twenty-four hours of duty time were reported." With adverse symptoms delimited *in advance*, there was little chance for a discovery of the broad range of possible vaccine effects.

## Soldiers Discouraged from Reporting Side Effects

Literalist doctors took this so far as to discourage soldiers from reporting illnesses when they didn't fit the bill as laid out in their instructions. The case of Air Force pilot Captain Michelle Piel illustrates this situation. After her first anthrax inoculation, her arm went numb. Some time later, her head filled with fluid. Her condition was so bad she was grounded.

Her doctor diagnosed this as a middle ear infection. When she got a second shot, she had the same numbness and symptoms of inner ear infection. Now, she suffered dizzy spells that kept her from driving and reading. The doctors decided to discontinue the anthrax shots. Hearing about the need for VAERS reports in such circumstances, she approached the chief flight surgeon, thinking he might help her fill one out. However, the "surgeon said her particular reaction[s] didn't fall within the criteria of reportable events." She voiced an understandable reaction. "It didn't make sense to me. . . . I was too sick to fly. I was too sick to get another shot. But my illness wasn't reportable on a VAERS form."

## No Records of Vaccines Were Allowed

Another feature of textbook-pure science is accurate record-keeping. How did the military do on that score? "In contrast to previous wars, service personnel were not allowed to keep a record of these vaccinations, and according to the DOD [Department of Defense] the shot records of hundreds of thousands of deployed personnel have since disappeared [said Nicolson]." Health personnel were threatened with court martial if they were found keeping their own records. Thus it would be difficult to know if there was a close connection between getting a shot and the onset of illness.

This was compounded by the fact that vaccines were not given according to Hoyle. . . .

From Nicolson's study:

> After passing their physical exams, they [military personnel preparing to go to the Gulf] received several types of vaccinations, mostly with commercially available vaccines. In the Persian Gulf area this was usually done by administering as many as two dozen vaccine doses over a period of a few days, even if the vaccines were normally required to be given over a course of several months to over a year.

As Nicolson and colleagues make clear, aside from flying in the face of scientific procedure and possibly erasing the positive disease-combating effects the vaccines might have, massive doses of vaccines "can result in immune depression and leave individuals susceptible to opportunistic infections, such as types the vaccine were supposed to protect against."

## Complaints Dismissed

In light of military physicians' ignorance of the full range of possible adverse side effects to the vaccine, it is not surprising that these doctors often pooh-poohed complaints of vaccinated men. A reporter for the *Cleveland Free Times* describes the case of local man Tom Colosimo, a seven-year Air Force vet, and former body builder, who was given anthrax inoculations from February 1998 to September 1999. The first shot made him feel dizzy and fatigued. After the second shot, he broke out with cysts on his face and head. "A doctor told him the cysts might be caused by sweat because Colosimo was working out so much." After taking his fourth shot, he was sent to Kuwait, where he felt nausea and chest pains. "In eight weeks, he shed forty pounds."

Back home, his physical deterioration became worse, with frequent blackouts and dizziness, leading to periods of hospitalization. Given that these symptoms weren't recognized as related to his vaccinations—remember Airwoman Piel also suffered dizziness, which her doctor said couldn't be ascribed to the vaccine—he "developed a reputation as a malingerer." Once when the police came to the base, responding to a call that Colosimo had collapsed, the police sergeant "said he was sick of playing games. . .and accused him of faking his illness."

Colosimo was eventually vindicated when the military admitted it was wrong about him. Marine Major General Randall West, in testimony before a House Subcommittee, stated, "Unfortunately the doctors do believe that. . .Colosimo's problems were caused by the anthrax vaccine." Yet, General West qualified his admission in this way, "Of all the people that were here today [various military personnel claiming to have suffered adverse effects from the vaccination] there was only one person who had a medical diagnosis that directly links it to the anthrax vaccine." This one person was Colosimo....

## Soldiers Punished

The military seems to have grown woefully lax in attending to medical matters. And when individuals call attention to problems and indiscrepancies, and where in a scientific atmosphere their grievances would be dispassionately assessed, in the prevailing military climate these complainants bear a punitive brunt. We saw that in how, at first, Colosimo was branded a malingerer. Two more recent cases show the same intolerance on the part of defense authorities who refuse to entertain any objections to orders.

In October 2000, Captain John Buck, a military doctor stationed at Kessler Air Force base in Mississippi, refused to take anthrax inoculations. He gave as his reasons, "I view this as an investigational vaccine being used in an off-label fashion." That is, to his mind, there was wholesale administration of a vaccine that had never been adequately tested. Buck argued further, that if, as an officer, he understood the necessity of following orders, as a doctor, he appreciated the importance of respecting patients' rights and testing drugs on a small sample before exposing a large population to it. Buck was facing court martial for his stance. Whatever his fate as of January 2002, *102 military personnel had already been court-martialed* for refusing vaccination.

Earlier in the year, Air Force Major Sonnie Bates from Dover Air Force base in Delaware took the same position by refusing anthrax vaccine. His unwillingness to get vaccinated was not based in medical scruple, but more pragmatic concerns. According to a news report on the Optimal Wellness Web site, "medical records obtained by CBS News [which was doing a piece on Bates's case] show that more than one hundred service members [at his base] reported the vaccine made them ill. Some pilots became so sick they were grounded." As in the Colosimo incident, charges flew that those who became sick were simply trying to escape duty. Moreover, Bates reports that other personnel came to him, saying, "Major, the doctor told me if I talk about anthrax that I'll be facing medical discharge."

Bates grounded his worries in what he understood about military boondoggles. He knew the one plant making the vaccine had been repeatedly cited for safety violations, and, as he put it, "There is a difference between being willing to give your life and sacrificing your health over a mismanaged government contract."

## Worries about Vaccine Maker

The plant Bates was alarmed about is owned by BioPort, which is located in Lansing, Michigan. The facility had been in the possession of the state, but was so plagued with safety problems that the government unloaded it in 1997. The group that bought the factory was headed by Fuad El-Hibri, a German-born businessman of Lebanese extraction who is now a United States citizen. Some improprieties were suspected in that two weeks after BioPort took over the biological establishment, the firm signed a contract with the Pentagon for $45 million to supply anthrax vaccine (called AVA). According to journalist Julie Klotter, the suspicions about the firm were based on the fact that retired Admiral William Crowe, Jr., who had been head of the Joint Chiefs of Staff as well as Ambassador to Britain—El-Hibri had owned a British biological corporation—"was given 12 percent to 13 percent of the company in exchange for a 'token amount' and BioPort's use of his name."

It has been reported that Admiral Crowe had been lobbying the DoD in El-Hibri's behalf from the beginning.

As with so many Pentagon contracts, there were cost overruns. According to Klotter, in 1999, the government granted BioPort an additional $24.1 million for the original contract and upped the payment for individual doses from 200 percent to 500 percent for fewer doses.

## No Exclusive Studies to Indicate Safety

Although these seemingly shady goings-on give one pause, they are not germane to the major question being raised here: Is the anthrax vaccine safe? We should begin by being clear that, as the CDC [Centers for Disease Control and Prevention] notices, the few studies that have been done, give AVA a clean bill of health. One report looked at the reactions of inoculees to the vaccine during the Korean War. "Most reported [adverse health] events were localized, minor and self limited," with only 0.3 percent experiencing a full day's loss from duty. AS to long-term ill effects, which the Korean War study did not look into, an examination of workers at the United States biowarfare base at Fort Derrick (who have to be inoculated for germs they are working with) found there were no unusual illnesses or conditions associated with AVA over a long time span. Lastly, two studies of Gulf War veterans who had been given the vaccine showed "no association" between taking the anthrax vaccination and Gulf War syndrome.

These studies have been positive, although one can't help remarking on the paucity of examinations of a vaccine that is being distributed so widely in the armed forces. As Captain Buck noted, it seems unwise to use a drug so widely on which only a few studies have been done. Moreover, a different examination of the effect of the vaccine on the Gulf War military, cited in the Cleveland paper, looked at Kansas City veterans and "found that 34 percent of those who were vaccinated and deployed met the definition for Gulf War syndrome, compared to 4 percent of Gulf War-era veterans who were not deployed and did not receive the vaccine." On top of that, 12 percent of veterans who were not sent to the theater of war but who *did* receive the vaccine came down with the Gulf War medical condition. This, let us note, is far from solid proof that the syndrome is tied to the vaccination, in that there are many other factors that may play a part in generation of the disease condition. We can say, however, that evidence on the implication of the anthrax vaccine in short- and long-term illness is inconclusive at best.

You might note, by the way, that the vaccine was approved in 1970 before tests to meet FDA approval were required. According to Nicolson, "in the case of the anthrax vaccine, long-term safety date were not supplied with the license application, and none has as yet been supplied to the FDA."

## Untested Adjuvants

Vaccines are often produced with weakened or dead germs of the disease to be guarded against. AVA itself doesn't use whole anthrax bacteria but cellular bits from the B. *anthracis* that are found in edemal (intercellular) fluid of infected animals. This doesn't mean that these bits are directly injected into the blood, because the germ—and this is the case with all vaccines—has to be carried by different agents in the vaccine, called "adjuvants." In AVA, the major adjuvant is aluminum hydroxide.

According to author Walene James, there are some researchers who feel agents such as aluminum hydroxide may themselves cause a problem. Nonetheless, an outcry around the preparation used to safeguard Gulf War troops turns not on the adjuvant that have been authorized but on the possibility that unapproved ones were added. In fact, an investigation by Congressman Jack Metcalf (assisted by the federal government's General Accounting Office or GAO), revealed in a hearing held in November 2001 that squalene, an oil used in the processing of cholesterol, was found in tested anthrax vaccine. It was suggested that this oil might have also appeared in the vaccine given to those going into battle in the Gulf War. What is at issue is not that squalene causes some particular problem, but that as an untested additive, no one knows what squalene's effect might be.

Metcalf's investigation took three years, partly because of the obstructive attitude of the Defense Department. "GAO also found Peter Collis, DOD official who headed vaccine efforts, refused to cooperate with them." Overall, the GAO found "a pattern of deception," with the Pentagon changing its story whenever it was faced with evidence that former stories didn't hold water.

## Expired, Ineffective Vaccines

Not only has military authority been charged with trying out experimental versions of the vaccine, ones laced with an untried adjuvant, but it has been further accused of being in such a hurry to get its forces inoculated that it used outdated medicines. Given the outcry around the use of the vaccine, in 1998 some of the remaining lots from AVA used to inoculate the troops were tested. Only six out of thirty-one lots retested were potent. Partially this was because the vaccine had expired. However, it was still being treated by the military as if were ready for use, and the lots had been redated once it had expired, not only once but sometimes twice, after a second expiration. "The question was raised whether expired or failed vaccine lots were used for vaccinating military personnel during the Gulf War," according to Nicolson, as it seemed to be, standard procedure was to keep redating vaccines (perhaps so they wouldn't go to waste), then it is not unlikely—and this is what the researchers retesting the vaccine concluded—that out-of-date and hence ineffective vaccines were given to the fighting troops.

Aside from these possible problems with the vaccine, there is the further question of whether, even in its approved stale, it would be effective against the type of anthrax a germ warfare-toting opponent is likely to throw at our military. As already noted, the most effective route for spreading anthrax is via airborne spores. Soldiers breathing in the bacteria would contract inhalational anthrax, the deadliest form of the infection. This is the type of infection that recently killed a reporter, two postal employees, and a New York hospital worker. However, the vaccine has not proven itself against this form of the disease. "According to Kevin Hoffman in the *Cleveland Free Times*, A study of an earlier anthrax vaccine ... found that it protected humans against anthrax absorbed through the skin, but could not determine its efficacy against inhaled anthrax."

## Russian Doll Cocktail

Let's say, for the time being, that AVA could cope with inhalational anthrax. Even then, the vaccine would only be useful against straw enemies who had nothing in their arsenal except the simple airborne spores. As the group Doctors for Disaster Preparedness point out, "An additional threat in the context of biological warfare is the potential use of genetically engineered strains, against which both vaccine and antibiotics may be ineffective." We now know that both Soviet biowarfare and Iraqi laboratories developed new, more potent strains of anthrax. Further, it seems only the most unsophisticated enemy would rely on one germ for its attack. The weapon of choice now is the so-called "Russian Doll Cocktail." According to Nicolson, "this is an aerosolized BW and chemical mixture that is designed to inhibit and overwhelm the body's defensive abilities." Not only would such a cocktail contain more than one disease agent, but it would enclose a number of drugs that weaken immunity, allowing the diseases a freer hand. . . .

Let us end this section by returning to the question of the Gulf War syndrome (also known as Gulf War Illnesses to indicate their may be more than one disease involved here). This condition is characterized by chronic fatigue, headaches, nausea, cognitive and gastrointestinal dysfunctions, fever, joint aches, muscle pains and other symptoms, The jury is still out

## Hold Anthrax Vaccine to Highest Standards

This submission to the [Food and Drug Administration] FDA simply asks one thing of the agency: use valid science to assure safety and efficacy before approving the anthrax vaccine license. Unfortunately, FDA has shown a bias toward ignoring the science in its vaccine regulatory decisions. . . .

FDA's history of regulatory malfeasance [wrongdoing] with respect to anthrax vaccine, combined with the emergency use provision of the 2004 BioShield Act, create the scenario for an anthrax vaccine disaster that affects a much larger segment of the U.S. population, and not just the military.

*Meryl Nass, Vera Sharov, Barbara Loe Fisher, and Steve Robinson,*
*"Comments and Questions Regarding FDA's proposed rule*
*and order to license Anthrax Vaccine Adsorbed."* Alliance
For Human Research Protection *March 29, 2005. Available at*
*http://ahrp/org/ahrpspeaks/anthraxFDAcomments0305.pdf.*

on what is behind this medical condition, and the correlative study we noted, which sought to link anthrax inoculations to the syndrome, was nor convincing. However, we should think about what we mentioned earlier about the way multiple immunizations weaken the immune system, and some say this is behind the syndrome. This point would not make AVA alone responsible for the illness, but rather a contributor that works in conjunction with all the other vaccines passed out. If we tie this to reports on the anthrax vaccine by British Gulf War veterans, the only group that did test the vaccines used on the troops, which found the vaccine was contaminated with unknown microorganisms, we might agree with Dr. Nicolson and his colleagues, who suspect that the anthrax vaccine (along with others given in such haste) had *a part* to play in causing the syndrome. Note well, the Nicolson study does not lay the whole illness at the door of AVA or any of the other administered vaccines, but simply sees it and them as vital contributing factors.

At the moment, these problems with AVA are of most concern to military personnel since they are ones who, even today, face vaccinations as preparation for going into battle against bioweapon-armed foes.

# Periodical Bibliography

*The following articles have been selected to supplement the diverse views presented in this chapter.*

| | |
|---|---|
| Bonnie Brewer Cavanaugh | "Thompson: Strengthen Public Health System," *Best's Review*. December, 2006. |
| Anita Cicero | "So How's Our BioShield?" *Legal Times*. October 8, 2007. |
| Kurt B. Copper | "'High and Dry?': The Public Readiness and Emergency Preparedness Act and Liability Protection for Pharmaceutical Manufacturers," *Journal of Health Law*. Winter, 2007. |
| James Dornbrook | "Feds Protect Food Supply With Stringer Laws," *Kansas City Business Journal*. September 8, 2006. |
| Meredith Hobbs | "On The Record: Bad Image Lingers for Speaker," *Fulton County Daily Report*. September 10, 2007. |
| Rima E. Laibow | "The Syringe of Death: Coming Soon to a Police Station Near You," *HealthFreedomUSA.org*, 2005. Available at www.healthfreedomusa.org. |
| Angie C. Marek | "A Meager Yield from BioShield," *U.S. News & World Report*. March 26, 2007. |
| National Institute of Allergy and Infectious Diseases | "The Need for Biosafety Laboratory Facilities," Available at www.niaid.nih.gov. September, 2007. |
| Wendy E. Parmet | "Legal and Legal Rights—Isolation and Quarantine in the Case of Drug Resistant Tuberculosis," *New England Journal of Medicine*. August 2, 2007. |
| Joby Warrick | "The Secretive Fight Against Bioterror," *Washington Post*. July 30, 2006. |

# For Further Discussion

## Chapter 1

1. Jason Pate and Gary Ackerman believe the bioterrorism threat is real and imminent, while Milton Leitenberg believes there are other more pressing threats than bioterrorism. What do you think each author perceives is the ability of terrorists to work with pathogens, and how is this related to his belief about the threat of bioterrorism?

2. Kevin Coleman asserts that the U.S. food supply chain is vulnerable to a terrorist attack and Rocco Casagrande, contends that a bioterrorist attack on the nation's agricultural sector would severely cripple the U.S. economy. What are the differences and similarities between Coleman's and Casagrande's arguments?

3. Richard Farmer thinks the agricultural industry would be able to respond to disruptions and keep economic losses relatively small in the event of a bioterrorist attack. What does Farmer have to say about government programs and food safety?

## Chapter 2

1. Rona Hirschberg, John La Montagne, and Anthony Fauci talk about biodefense laboratories, as does Laura Kahn. However, their two viewpoints express very different perceptions of these laboratories. Why do you think Hirschberg, La Montagne, and Fauci may have different perceptions than Kahn? Explain.

2. Bioterrorism Watch editors note that many of the same health-care issues are raised regardless of whether health-care workers are responding to a bioterrorist attack or a pandemic flu outbreak. They contend that the 1918 flu

pandemic provides lessons for flu preparedness and bioterrorism. Name three of these lessons. What might Barton Reppert think about government-funded research to study the 1918 flu pandemic?

3. The Agency for Healthcare Research and Quality concluded that smallpox poses a threat to public health that could cause widespread casualties and that communities should prepare. However, George J. Annas asserts that use of the smallpox vaccine is not justified by the vague fears of bioterrorism put forth by the U.S. government. How do you think each would rate the risk of a bioterrorist incident using smallpox as a weapon? Compare their perceptions of the risk of a smallpox bioterrorist incident with their perception of the risk of smallpox vaccination.

# Chapter 3

1. Hillel Cohen, Robert Gould, and Victor Sidel contend that bioterrorism preparedness programs have harmed public health. What do these authors believe are the greatest root causes of worldwide mortality and morbidity, and the underlying cause of terrorism? Do you think the authors believe that bioterrorism preparedness programs are a good investment? Explain.

2. What is dual use research, and what do you think Charles Schable thinks about it?

3. Edward Richards, Katharine Rathbun, and Jay Gold describe a situation in which everyone is clamoring for a vaccine after a disease outbreak. But Ira Longini and Elizabeth Halloran say mass vaccination is not necessary and they would only vaccinate health-care workers and the close contacts of infected individuals. Based on the author's arguments, who do you most agree with? Would you want or not want the vaccine? Why or why not? Use supporting or opposing arguments from the viewpoints.

4. The U.S. Department of Health and Human Services (HHS) says the nation is better prepared to respond to a bioterrorist incident, while Trust for America's Health believes the public health system is not prepared to handle such an incident. How does it appear that each author measured preparedness? What did they look at? Explain.

## Chapter 4

1. President George W. Bush believes that Project BioShield will encourage pharmaceutical companies to develop new medicines that will protect Americans against bioterrorism. But Debora MacKenzie says the pharmaceutical industry has not responded to BioShield incentives. Why do you think pharmaceutical companies need incentives to make remedies for rare diseases, like the diseases caused by biological weapons?

2. What reasons do Michael Mair, Beth Maldin, and Brad Smith give for why they believe the Pandemic and All-Hazards Preparedness Act will improve public health? What reasons does OMB Watch provide for their disapproval of the exemptions from the Freedom of Information Act given to the Preparedness Act? Do you agree or disagree with each author? Whose viewpoint do you believe is better supported? Explain.

3. The Military Vaccine Agency says that anthrax poses a serious threat and service members should be vaccinated against it. However, Gary Null and James Feast say there are too many problems with the anthrax vaccine and service members should not be required to take it. Whose viewpoint do you agree with and why?

# Organizations to Contact

*The editors have compiled the following list of organizations concerned with the issues debated in this book. The descriptions are derived from materials provided by the organizations. All have publications or information available for interested readers. The list was compiled on the date of publications of the present volume; the information provided here may change. Be aware that many organizations may take several weeks or longer to respond to inquiries, so allow as much time as possible.*

**Association of State and Territorial**
**Health Officials (ASTHO)**
2231 Crystal Dr., Suite 450, Arlington, VA    22202
(202) 371-9090 • fax: (571) 527-3189
Web site: http://astho.org

The Association of State and Territorial Health Officials (ASTHO) is a national nonprofit organization representing the state and territorial public health agencies of the United States, the U.S. territories, and the District of Columbia. ASTHO works to formulate and influence sound public health policy, particularly regarding bioterrorism preparedness. The organization publishes newsletters, survey results, resource lists, and policy papers that assist states in the development of bioterrorism preparedness and other policies.

**Bradford Disarmament Research Centre**
University of Bradford, Bradford, West Yorkshire    BD7 1DP
+44 (0)1274 23 2323
e-mail: course-enquiries@bradford.ac.uk
Web site: or http://www.brad.ac.uk/acad/bdrc/

The Bradford Disarmament Research Centre, Department of Peace Studies, is an international center of academic and policy-oriented research on the proliferation and control of nuclear, biological, chemical, and conventional weapons. The

Centre administers the Biological and Toxin Weapons Convention (BWC) Web site (www.opbw.org/), which provides accurate, up-to-date information about the BWC. The Centre also publishes various research reports and studies on biological, chemical, and nuclear disarmament.

### Center for Arms Control and Nonproliferation

Hans Bethe Center, Washington, DC   20036
(202) 546-0795 ext. 107
e-mail: apearson@armscontrolcenter.org
Web site: http://www.armscontrolcenter.org

The Center for Arms Control and Nonproliferation is a nonprofit, nonpartisan policy organization that is dedicated to enhancing international peace and security and protecting American people from the threat of weapons of mass destruction. The Center seeks to reduce and ultimately eliminate nuclear weapons and halt the spread of all weapons of mass destruction, including biological weapons. Staff at the organization provide commentary and analysis published in newspapers and journals throughout the world.

### Center for Biosecurity

The Center for Biosecurity of UPMC; The Pier IV Building
621 E. Pratt St., Suite 210, Baltimore, MD   21202
(443) 573-3304 • fax: (443) 573-3305
Web site: www.upmc-biosecurity.org/

The Center for Biosecurity is an independent, nonprofit organization of the University of Pittsburgh Medical Center. The Center for Biosecurity works to change public policy in order to lessen the illness, death, and civil disruption that would follow a large-scale biological attack or a natural epidemic. The organization publishes several journals including *Biosecurity and Bioterrorism, Clinicians' Biosecurity Network Current,* and *Biosecurity Briefing.*

## Centers for Disease Control and Prevention (CDC)
1600 Clifton Rd., Atlanta, GA   30333
(404) 639-3311
Web site: www.cdc.gov

The U.S. Centers for Disease Control and Prevention (CDC) is the main health agency of the United States government. The mission of the CDC is to promote health and quality of life by preventing and controlling disease, injury, and disability. The CDC provides up-to-date information to the public on health and diseases. The agency publishes several journals including *Emerging Infectious Diseases* and *Morbidity and Mortality Weekly Report.*

## Defense Science Board
The Pentagon; OUSD (AT&L) Rm. 3C553
Washington, DC   20310
(703) 695-4157
Web site: www.acq.osd.mil/dsb/

The U.S. Defense Science Board, created by the U.S. government in 1956, seeks to use newly acquired scientific knowledge and technologies in order to help defend the United States against enemy attacks. The Board, composed of U.S. scientists, advises the U.S. Department of Defense (DoD) on ways to defend the U.S. against biological, chemical, and nuclear warfare and helps to ensure the DoD takes advantage of revolutionary new technologies. The DSB publishes a quarterly newsletter and various in-depth reports.

## Federation for American Scientists (FAS)
1717 K St., NW; Suite 209, Washington, DC   20036
(202) 546-3300 • fax: (202) 675-1010
e-mail: webmaster@fas.org
Web site: www.fas.org

The Federation for American Scientists (FAS) is an international, nonprofit organization composed of scientists and engineers who promote humanitarian uses of science and technology. The FAS seeks to provide the public, media, and policy makers with high-quality information to better inform debates about science-related issues, including the proliferation of biological weapons. The organization publishes the *FAS Public Interest Report, the FAS Occasional Paper,* and issues various reports.

**Henry L. Stimson Center**
1111 Nineteenth St.; 12th Fl., Washington, DC  20036
(202) 223-5956 • fax: (202) 238-9604
e-mail: webmaster@stimson.org
Web site: www.stimson.org

The Henry L. Stimson Center is a nonprofit, nonpartisan institution devoted to enhancing international peace and security through analysis and outreach. The Stimson Center focuses on reducing weapons of mass destruction, strengthening institutions for international peace and security, and building regional security. The Center publishes various books, reports, commentaries, and background papers.

**James Martin Center for Nonproliferation Studies (CNS)**
460 Pierce St., Monterey, CA  93940
(831) 647-4154 • fax: (831) 647-3519
e-mail: cns@miis.edu
Web site: http://cns.miis.edu

The James Martin Center for Nonproliferation Studies (CNS) seeks to combat the spread of weapons of mass destruction through education, analysis, and public outreach. The CNS is located at the Monterey Institute of International Studies and is the largest nongovernmental organization in the United States devoted exclusively to research and training on nonproliferation issues. The organization publishes several periodical journals, including the *Nonproliferation Review* and the *International Export Control Observer.*

## National Institute of Allergy and Infectious Diseases (NIAID)

NIAID Office of Communications and Public Liaison
6610 Rockledge Dr., MSC 6612, Bethesda, MD   20892-6612
(866) 284-4107 • fax: (301) 402-3573

The National Institute of Allergy and Infectious Diseases (NIAID) is an agency within the U.S. Department of Health and Human Services. NIAID conducts and supports basic and applied research to better understand, treat, and ultimately prevent infectious, immunologic, and allergic diseases. The agency issues several publications, briefs, and reports on infectious diseases and biodefense.

## Nuclear Threat Initiative (NTI)

1747 Pennsylvania Avenue NW, 7th Fl.
Washington, DC   20006
(202) 296-4810 • fax: (202) 296-4811
e-mail: contact@nti.org
Web site: www.nti.org

The Nuclear Threat Initiative (NTI) is a nonprofit organization with a mission to strengthen global security by reducing the risk of use and preventing the spread of nuclear, biological and chemical weapons, and to work to build the trust, transparency, and security which are preconditions to the ultimate fulfillment of the Non-Proliferation Treaty's goals and ambitions.

## Sunshine Project

Edward Hammond; PO Box 41987, Austin, TX   78704
(512) 494-0545
e-mail: Hammond@sunshine-project.org
Web site: www.sunshine-project.org

The Sunshine Project is an international nonprofit organization that seeks to stop the use of biological weapons. The organization also opposes smallpox research and advocates for the eradication of the smallpox virus. The organization publishes various briefs and backgrounders.

**Trust for America's Health (TFAH)**
1707 H Street, NW; 7th Fl., Washington, DC   20006
(202) 223-9870 • fax: (202) 223-9871
e-mail: info@tfah.org
Web site: www.tfah.org

Trust for America's Health (TFAH) is a nonprofit, nonpartisan organization dedicated to protecting the health of Americans and working to make disease prevention a national priority. The organization focuses on protecting Americans from bioterrorism and natural epidemics. TFAH publishes several reports and online information guides.

**World Health Organization (WHO)**
Avenue Appia 20, Geneva 27   CH - 1211
   Switzerland
+41 22 791 2111 • fax: +41 22 791 3111
e-mail: info@who.int
Web site: www.who.int

The World Health Organization (WHO) is the directing and coordinating authority for health within the United Nations system. It is responsible for providing leadership on global health matters, shaping the health research agenda, setting norms and standards, articulating evidence-based policy options, providing technical support to countries, and monitoring and assessing health trends.

# Bibliography

## Books

Arthur Allen  *Vaccine: The Controversial Story of Medicine's Greatest Lifesaver.* New York: W.W. Norton, 2007.

Daniel Barenblatt  *A Plague Upon Humanity: The Hidden History of Japan's Biological Warfare Program.* New York: HarperCollins, 2005.

Frances A. Boyle  *Biowarfare and Terrorism.* Atlanta, GA: Clarity Press: December, 2005.

Jennifer Brower and Peter Chalk  *The Global Threat of New and Re-emerging Infectious Diseases.* Santa Monica, CA: Rand Corporation, 2003.

Dan Caldwell and Robert E. Williams  *Seeking Security in an Insecure World.* Lanham, MD: Rowman & Littlefield Publishers, 2006.

Peter Chalk  *Hitting America's Soft Underbelly: The Potential Threat of Deliberate Biological Attacks Against the U.S. Agricultural and Food Industry.* Santa Monica, CA: Rand Corporation, 2004.

Joseph Cirincione, Jon B. Wolfsthal, and Miriam Rajkumar  *Deadly Arsenals: Nuclear, Biological, and Chemical Threats.* Washington, D.C.: Carnegie Endowment for International Peace, 2005.

| | |
|---|---|
| Anthony H. Cordesman | *The Challenge of Biological Terrorism.* Washington D.C.: CSIS Press, December 2005. |
| Eric Croddy and James J. Wirtz | *Weapons of Mass Destruction: An Encyclopedia of Worldwide Policy, Technology, and History.* Santa Barbara, CA: ABC-CLIO, 2005. |
| Clive and Dirk Cussler | *Black Wind.* New York: G.P. Putnam's Sons, 2004. |
| Lynn E. Davis, Tom LaTourrette, David E. Mosher, Lois M. Davis, and David R. Howell | *Individual Preparedness and Response to Chemical, Radiological, Nuclear, and Biological Terrorist Attacks.* Santa Monica, CA: Rand Corporation, 2003. |
| Janet Decker | *Deadly Diseases and Epidemics: Anthrax.* Philadelphia: Chelsea House Publishers, 2003. |
| I.W. Fong and Ken Alibek | *Bioterrorism and Infectious Agents: A New Dilemma for the 21st Century.* New York: Springer, 2005. |
| Sean M. Grady and John Tabak | *Biohazards: Humanity's Battle With Infectious Disease.* New York: Facts On File, 2006. |
| Robert Graysmith | *Amerithrax: The Hunt for the Anthrax Killer.* New York: Jove Books, 2003. |
| Michael L. Gross | *Bioethics and Armed Conflict: Moral Dilemmas of Medicine and War.* Cambridge, MA: MIT Press, 2006. |

Jeanne Guillemin *Biological Weapons: From the Invention of State-Sponsored Programs to Contemporary Bioterrorism.* New York: Columbia University Press, 2005.

Sam Harris *The End of Faith: Religion, Terror, and the Future of Reason.* New York: W.W. Norton & Co., 2004.

Kathiann M. Kowalski *Attack of the Superbugs: The Crisis of Drug-Resistant Diseases.* Berkeley Heights, NJ: Enslow Publishers, 2005.

Milton Leitenberg *The Problem of Biological Weapons.* Stockholm, Sweden: Swedish National Defense College, 2004.

Kurt Link *Understanding New, Resurgent, and Resistant Diseases: How Man and Globalization Create and Spread Illness.* Westport, CT: Praeger Publishers, 2007.

Jonathan D. Moreno *In the Wake of Terror.* Cambridge, MA: MIT Press, 2003.

John Mueller *Overblown: How Politicians and the Terrorism Industry Inflate National Security Threats, and Why We Believe Them.* New York: Simon & Schuster, Free Press, 2006.

Marion Nestle *Safe Food: Bacteria, Biotechnology, and Bioterrorism.* Berkeley, CA: University of California Press, 2003.

Gary Null with James Feast — *Germs, Biological Warfare, Vaccinations: What You Need to Know.* New York: Seven Stories Press, 2003.

Richard F. Pilch and Raymond A. Zilinskas — *Encyclopedia of Bioterrorism Defense.* Hoboken, NJ: Wiley-LISS, 2005.

Mark Sauter and James Jay Carafano — *Homeland Security: A Complete Guide to Understanding, Preventing, and Surviving Terrorism.* New York: McGraw-Hill, 2005.

United States Congress House Committee on Homeland Security — *Engineering Bio-Terror Agents: Lessons from the Offensive U.S. and Russian Biological Weapons Programs: Hearing before the Subcommittee on Prevention of Nuclear and Biological Attack, July 13, 2005.* Washington: U.S. GPO, 2006.

Mark Wheelis, Rózsa, Lajos, and Malcom Dando — *Deadly Cultures: Biological Weapons Since 1945.* Cambridge, Mass.: Harvard University Press, 2006.

Geoffrey L. Zubay — *Agents of Bioterrorism: Pathogens and Their Weaponization.* New York: Columbia University Press, 2005.

# Index